STORIES OF FAITH AND COURAGE FROM GOD AND OPEN ROAD ADVENTURES

STORIES OF FAITH AND COURAGE FROM GOD AND OPEN ROAD ADVENTURES

TIM RITER

GOD & COUNTRY™
PRESS

Stories of Faith and Courage from God and Open Road Adventures

Published by AMG Publishers, Chattanooga, TN

Italicized type in Scripture added by author, for emphasis.

Print Edition ISBN 13: 978-1-61715-628-1

Manuscript editing by Marissa Wold Uhrina, Eden Prairie, MN
Text design and layout by PerfecType, Nashville, TN
Printed in the United States of America

POD

CONTENTS

DAY ONE

GETTING INTO IT: THE MIRACLES OF MOTORCYCLES AND SPORTS CARS

"Ride majestically! Ride triumphantly!
Ride on the side of truth!
Ride for the righteous meek!"
Psalm 45:3–4 (MSG)

From my earliest memories, fast cars fascinated me. I grew up with Dad telling stories of his world-record Cannonball Run for crossing the United States from New York City to Santa Monica. He and Babe Hutchings, a friend and fellow employee at the Heinickle Ford dealer in Santa Monica, bought a 1929 Ford Model A Roadster, drove it to New York to start at 12:00 a.m. May 28, 1929, and arrived at the Santa Monica Pier on June 1, traveling 3,364 miles in 77 hours . . . and two minutes. I still pull out the papers every so often.

Around 1958, our family crossed the Nevada desert, then with no speed limit, and Dad wanted to see what his 1955 Ford Fairlane 500 with a V-8 could do. Leaving Tonopah, he got it up to 120 and kept it at 95 to 110, until he ran out of gas seven miles shy of Ely. Mom pretended to sleep with my sister in the back seat, while I sat in the front and grinned the whole time.

And it seemed that in high school when we hitchhiked to Huntington Beach to body surf, the classic mid-'60s Jaguar XKEs filled the road. Few cars embodied their grace and lines.

Soon came my direct encounters. While delivering truck parts around SoCal, my dispatcher Jim had me test drive sports cars he was interested in. Corvettes, Porches, the then-new Datsun 240Z, and more. A Lotus Elan, a race-bred sports car, topped the list, and when Jim declined it, I almost bought it myself. The grip while accelerating on the corners amazed me.

But my ultimate car experience came when my wife gifted me with driving a Lamborghini Gallardo 550 at Exotics Raceway at the AAA road course in Fontana. Seven laps and 8.4 miles with 56 turns, a top speed of 112 that felt like 200. You'll come across a lot of these stories in this book and my blog, *Unconventional*, at timriter.com.

Getting into motorcycles took more time; I just never thought of them. Then in the fall of my senior year in college, a neighbor almost forced me to try his kids' Honda Trail 90. Just to shut him up, I did. Nice. Not captivating. But nice.

Near the end of that year, my roommate Mark and I planned on taking my 1964 Ford Falcon to Canada to visit another friend—but things began to change. Mark ran out of money for the trip, and a lady ran into my Falcon on a Los Angeles freeway. I didn't feel confident driving it that far, and the trip evaporated.

During finals week, several of us got tired of studying and headed for a local theater to see *Easy Rider*, the iconic cult film depicting sex, drugs, and bikes. It entranced me. Not with the sex and drugs, although I certainly wasn't walking with Jesus then. But Peter Fonda and Dennis Hopper captured a freedom of traveling on two wheels that captivated me.

The idea burst on me like inspiration—I'd work for a month or so, save enough to buy a bike, and head to Canada for a month before grad school started.

DAY ONE

I bought what I could afford: a 1970 Honda 350 Scrambler, a cross between a road and dirt bike. Much too small for such a trip. Much too multipurpose for a long tour. Three weeks after the purchase, I took off. Much too soon for a rookie rider. I returned, barely, for the start of grad school, but more importantly, I graduated into motorcycling. I discovered how a motorcycle could lead to a miracle of a transformed life.

Fifty-five years have passed, and 270,000 miles have accumulated on my odometers, reaching all 50 states, DC, Canada, and Mexico. Those miles have brought enough stories for two biker devotions and now this, *God and Open Road Adventures*. Devotions for lovers of the open road, for bikers and sports car drivers.

Motorcycles and sports cars share common passions: curvy roads, the open air, and responsive vehicles. They're sometimes used for commuting, but they fulfill their purpose when we get away on open roads—they feed our souls' desire for adventure in the marriage of driver, vehicle, and road.

I began following Jesus at 11, until the shallowness of my faith led to four years of questioning and searching in college. Ironically, although I didn't follow Jesus then, that first Canada trip played a key role in me coming back to God. I've been with him ever since. I've pastored churches and written books about living as a Jesus follower.

Devotions? Yes, but a bit more. Not so much affirming as challenging. They will challenge you to blend Jesus in your life as well, however you ride. The Days may contain questions that cause you to think of riding—or Christianity—in a new light.

Use them as best fits you. If you're in a group, choose to read one at a meeting and kick it around a bit. Or if you're on a ride, start the day with one. Give the book away to fellow riders who may not yet know Jesus, or gift it for Christmas. This book is not an evangelistic tract, but it might help them see Jesus in a fresh way. And as you read, you'll notice some Days are written by other fellow riders and lovers of sports cars, friends who have fine stories to tell. They tell their stories; I wrote the application.

Crossing the Finish Line

What's your experience with vehicles that thrill you? A lot of both bikes and sports cars, or one or the other? Never? Occasional rides on both? Thinking about getting into these? What intrigues you about them? What about them makes you uneasy?

Whatever your background, I'm glad you hopped on for the adventure. I hope you enjoy the stories and are touched by the applications.

DAY TWO

THE LAST RIDE: SAYING GOODBYE TO STUFF WE LOVE

How tight is our grip on the things we love? Cars. Boats. Houses. Activities. And more. The stuff of life. Reality caught up with me in 2020. The bike I'd loved and ridden all over the West was no longer the right bike for me with my changing body at 72. My ST1300 sport tourer was fast, comfortable, and matched me like a fitted suit—the best bike for how I rode. It gave me an Iron Butt ride at my age of 70, covering 1,080 miles in 16.2 hours. That averages 68 miles per hour, including stops. Now, to be fair, most of the speed limit on I-15 was 80 miles per hour. I had some fine journeys with my riding buddies, both the Gray Hogs and others. But my balance and reactions had noticeably gotten worse, and I couldn't safely keep up with one particular younger friend on the mountain curves. My competitive streak still runs strong.

And I knew that I couldn't go slower on that bike; I would try to corner as fast as I used to, which couldn't be done safely. So to keep riding and stay alive, the realization came that the time had arrived to say goodbye. The day before the buyer would bring cash and take my bike, I took it out for one last ride. That last ride inspired these words.

A turn of a key
a push of a button
and the ST coughs once

catches, then purrs
too long neglected but forgiving
ready to roll for one last ride
Slipping out of town past the wineries
on country roads well ridden
memories accumulate
like the countless clouds on a blue sky
an Iron Butt of 1,080 miles in 16 hours
retracing an earlier trip to Canada
climbing to the sun in Glacier NP
laughs and stories shared with brothers on two wheels
with the conditions just right
seeing rubies behind as I ride to work
brisk air invigorates
bringing memories of frigid days
astride the bike
Twenty-eight for an hour's ride up to Jackson Hole
Eighteen degrees topping Deadman Pass on 395
A few photos
a lot of memories
Thank you, old friend

But as I helped the new owner load what was now his bike onto his trailer, and as he drove it away down my street and I took my last look at it, I surprisingly felt fine. No tears. No grief. Why? Every bike has given joy, yet when changing to the next, I moved on, wanting to enjoy the present and future and not get caught in the past. I like bikes but see them as a tool to enable riding; they are not jewels. Not something to cling to. And more deeply, I'm learning to keep a loose grip on the stuff of life. Why?

First, let's realize that God created an abundance of pleasurable options, ones he wants us to enjoy: "Moreover, when God gives someone wealth and possessions, and the *ability to enjoy them*, to accept their lot and be happy in their toil—*this is a gift of God*"

(Ecclesiastes 5:19). These possessions can include the biblically mentioned motorcycles in an older translation: "hear the Triumph . . . in the camp of the saved" (Psalm 118:15). Bad exegesis, but this makes me grin!

Second, stuff is temporary, with no guarantee we'll have it as long as we might wish. They wear out and break down. Our finances change. I lost my beloved '78 Goldwing 1000 after 30 years of riding when it broke down outside Sturgis, South Dakota, just before the big rally. Not a single shop there or in the next town could fix it for three months, so I had to swap it for a lesser bike to finish the trip. And nothing material lasts forever. They all will burn up: "That day will bring about the destruction of the heavens by fire, and the elements will melt in the heat" (2 Peter 3:12). Yes, stuff brings joy. Yes, we might have it on earth. But we can't take it with us.

Third, and most significantly, our stuff can distract us from what is most important in life, the one aspect that lasts: "So we fix our eyes not on what is seen, but on what is unseen, since what is seen is temporary, but what is unseen is eternal" (2 Corinthians 4:18). We humans, at least this human, can focus so much on the fun our stuff brings that we minimize our eternal life. We invest our resources and time in what doesn't last. Seems like a poor bargain to me.

Jesus taught about the difficulties the wealthy have in getting into heaven: Sometimes enjoying their stuff and getting more distracts them from the most important. And honestly, many Americans fit into this category; we are blessed materially. Yet that comes with a risk, an obsession with stuff can mean that "what sorrow awaits you who are rich, for you have your only happiness now" (Luke 6:24 NLT). And remember, accumulating wealth is not innately sinful; the wealthy have the opportunity for great generosity.

The problem: putting too much importance on stuff. Let's hold on to it with a loose grip.

Yes, I got another bike after the ST. An old man's bike, a beautiful and comfortable yellow Honda Goldwing. That bike took me to Alaska with Rich and to the East Coast with Jerry, and no other bike had been as comfortable and protected from the damp and heat and cold and wind. Then at the most dangerous intersection in Bridgeport, Connecticut, we hit a van. I got a small scrape; the Wing got totaled. Once more, I walked away . . . and got another. Still a Honda but a CTX1300 Deluxe. Similar to the ST but detuned. Not as fast. I'll ride as long as possible, as long as God wills. But I don't want bikes, or anything material, to get in between me and God.

Kick Starting the Application

What material item or activity most distracts you from intimacy with God? What causes that in you? How can you loosen the grip that your stuff has on you? How can you be more generous with your stuff?

DAY THREE

SPEED THRILLS: THE LESSONS OF FAST

Speed's Way

Two fingers pulled the paddle shifter; the Lamborghini Gallardo 550 slipped into gear and rolled up to the start line. A few seconds to check that the track was clear, and I took off, with my instructor Megan riding shotgun. Seven laps and 8.4 miles and 56 turns—together they thrilled me to the core of my soul.

By the time I pulled into the exit lane around 10 minutes later, I had passed a Lamborghini Huracan that had more horses than mine, took tight 160-degree turns at 80 miles per hour, and hit 112 on the straight. And I realized a long-time dream of driving a Lambo, a car I've admired since college days, decades back.

I enjoy going fast, particularly with previous vehicles like my Mustangs or my bikes, especially my earlier sport touring motorcycle, a Honda ST1300 that I took up to 130 miles per hour—something I have done a lot. But what I knew for those two didn't work in the Gallardo. My petite instructor Megan pushed me to push myself and the car to drive faster than I had ever imagined. Exotics Racing at the Auto Club Fontana Speedway helped me approach heaven.

Driving home, in our stable Honda Accord, I pondered the lessons on how to drive fast. A lot was counterintuitive—I had to fight my instincts to corner like I do in my Mustangs or my sport touring motorcycle. This Gallardo had so many more capabilities. I realized Megan knew far more about going fast than I. The more I listened and followed her commands, the faster I went. I'm still processing the experience and seeing new lessons.

God's Way

But I discovered that I had learned more than how to go fast. Those lessons about speed serve as a metaphor of following Jesus. Frankly, Jesus didn't tell us following him would be like a safe and stable Honda Accord. A Lamborghini sporting 550 horsepower, a top speed of 200 miles per hour, and a 0-to-60 time under 4 seconds better describes at least part of the journey. Listen to his description of what he expects to occur.

> "I am come that they might *have life*, and that they might have it more *abundantly*" (John 10:10 KJV).
>
> "Love the Lord your God with *all your heart* and with *all your soul* and with *all your mind* and with *all your strength*" (Mark 12:30).
>
> "I have come to bring *fire on the earth*, and how I wish it were already kindled! . . . Do you think I came to bring peace on earth? No, I tell you, but *division*" (Luke 12:49, 51).
>
> "If anyone comes to me and does not hate father and mother, wife and children, brothers and sisters—yes, even their own life—such a person cannot be my disciple. And whoever does not carry their cross and follow me cannot be my disciple. In the same way, those of you who do not give up everything you have cannot be my disciple" (Luke 14:26, 27, 33).
>
> "If the world hates you, keep in mind that it hated me first . . . If they persecuted me, they will persecute you also" (John 15:18, 20).

DAY THREE

Sounds like a wild, fun, difficult ride, doesn't it? And to be fair, the Honda Accord also works as a metaphor for the Christian life. But we often ignore the thrills and abundant life Jesus described, and that's the focus of our book. Maybe we need to begin to stretch ourselves spiritually as I stretched myself in the Lambo.

The speed thrills we get with bikes and sports cars could also be found in knowing him. I once had a small Toyota four-cylinder car for commuting; it served that purpose well, but it gave no thrills. Maybe we can up our game with faith. How? By being all in with God. In driving the Lambo, all my attention and concentration and energy focused on the car and the course. No daydreaming of laying out on a beach. I don't focus on God like I should.

Oh, he's the key part of my life, but many decisions don't involve him. I don't ask myself how to honor God in them all. At times, yes. Consistently, no. In Matthew 6:24–33, Jesus said we cannot serve both God and the material stuff of life, like food, drink, clothing, work, and more. The unbelievers chase the stuff; too often we try to do both. God recognizes our need for it but said it's a matter of priority. Which comes first?

Then in verse 33 he summarized how we prioritize the Creator of all and the stuff he made: "But *seek first* his kingdom and his righteousness, and *all these things* will be given to you as well."

Step one is that we analyze each decision: Will this lead me closer to God, his kingdom, and his righteousness, or away? We use the Bible to figure that out, not what others tell us, not what our desires tell us, not what tradition tells us but what does his Word says.

Then we put him first and do that, regardless of the consequences. Does a new job promotion require us to work on the weekends and miss fellowship and worship? Maybe we need to set that aside. And we do that, as best we can, with each turning point in life.

Then, and only then, do we get the thrills of a life wholly yielded to Jesus. Do we lose some stuff? Of course. But we get God and some stuff of life. And a fine ride along the way.

DAY THREE

Crossing the Finish Line

How much do you enjoy activities that thrill you? Do you appreciate watching those activities? What most intrigues you about motorcycles or sports cars? What vehicle that you've owned or driven most brought an adrenaline rush? How willing are you to stretch yourself spiritually to embark on fresh adventures? Maybe begin a ministry. Maybe try a more challenging one. Or can you hear the gentle whisper of the Spirit to make some character changes?

DAY FOUR

THE SWERVE TEST: NAVIGATING LIFE'S CHALLENGES

Cherie Denna

An author, pastor, and biker, Cherie's mission is to empower individuals to find a deep sense of belonging and belovedness in Jesus Christ. Cherie influences the world through writing, speaking, and women's ministry. Join the Everyday Belonging Movement at www.cheriedenna.com, and pick up Cherie's debut award-winning book, Beloved Outcast: The Quest for True Belonging.

Riding east on Highway 50 toward South Lake Tahoe on my 2000 Harley Davidson 1200 Sportster, the crisp, early-morning air rushed past, carrying the scent of pine and damp earth. There was light traffic on the road that stretched wide and open before me. A Kawasaki sport bike, a flash of green and chrome, trailed me in the center lane, while further ahead, a beat-up pickup truck carried a hazardous cargo—a hundred-plus steel bumpers, their shiny metal surfaces gleaming in the sun, stacked precariously high and held in place only by flimsy plywood sideboards.

Then it happened.

One of the sideboards gave way, and in an instant, chaos erupted. Metal bumpers shot across the freeway like missiles, bouncing unpredictably from lane to lane. Time seemed to slow. Life flashed before my eyes, and a scream caught in my throat. But then—clarity.

"The prudent see danger and take refuge, but the simple keep going and pay the penalty" (Proverbs 27:12).

Gripping the handlebars hard, I let off the throttle, creating space between me and the chaos ahead, my head ducked low to avoid impact. My training took over. Swerving left, then right, weaving through the airborne metal obstacles, I moved with precision. One wrong move, and it could have been the end.

Once the bumpers finally settled, I guided my bike to the median and stopped, my heart pounding in my chest. Breathe. Check for injuries. Check the tires. Miraculously, the bike and I were unscathed.

The Kawasaki rider pulled up beside me. "That was insane! You okay?"

I nodded, still catching my breath. "Yeah . . . that was a God thing. A big God thing."

Had it not been for my training—the countless hours preparing for the swerve test, learning how to anticipate danger and react swiftly—I might not have made it through. But more than that, it was God's wisdom, his unseen hand guiding me, that made the difference.

"Wisdom has built her house; she has hewn out her seven pillars" (Proverbs 9:1 ISV).

That day, I saw how life's challenges mirror that swerve test. We don't always see the obstacles coming, but God, in his wisdom, equips us to navigate them. The seven pillars of wisdom—reverence for God, knowledge, understanding, counsel, fortitude, righteousness, and discernment—are like the skills I had practiced on the course. They prepare us for the unexpected, keeping us steady when life blindsides us.

- Reverence for God reminds us that he is in control, even when chaos erupts.
- Knowledge and understanding teach us to recognize spiritual dangers before they escalate.
- Counsel and fortitude give us the strength to trust God and move wisely through trials.

- Righteousness and discernment keep us aligned with his will, helping us make decisions that lead to life, not destruction.

That day, I learned that faith isn't just for the quiet moments—it's for the swerves, the unexpected detours, the times when life hurls chaos our way.

And in those moments, wisdom is the difference between losing control and making it through.

In my 55 years of motorcycling, I've seen a lot of foolish riders, who ride beyond their skills or safety, who take unnecessary risks, who don't know their new bike enough. Add to that the issues like Cherie faced, and riding clearly provides a dangerous source of joy. My goal for all bikers, those heading to the local donut shop on a Saturday or taking off on a cross-country adventure, is that we arrive alive . . . with a smile. To accomplish that, we need some wisdom and preparation.

Cherie gave some great ways to prep for danger on rides, and her methods serve as metaphors for the spiritual life. We prepare. We build our knowledge base. We anticipate. We react wisely. So let's synthesize how we do that in following Jesus.

First, anticipate the reality of difficulties and dangers and disappointments. An early riding mentor suggested I look at every car on the road as intentionally out to get me. That works in life. Bad stuff and people abound, and we prepare ourselves with an awareness that at any time, anything can go sideways.

I like Peter's advice: "Dear friends, do not be surprised at the fiery ordeal that has come on you to test you, as though something strange were happening to you" (1 Peter 4:12). Yet we tend to expect easy lives, for life to go our way. Have you noticed that when bad stuff happens, we get surprised?

So as we do with riding, spiritually we craft a mindset to continually stay aware of what's going on, of how to respond. I like the all-encompassing principle that faith should be woven into all dimensions of life: "Everything that does not come from faith is sin" (Romans 14:23). Do we examine everything for possible spiritual impacts, like Cherie with the load of astray bumpers?

Jesus faced perhaps the greatest temptations of all time: When weakened by 40 days of fasting in the wilderness, he faced Satan himself, who hit him in mankind's most vulnerable areas of ego, physical desires, and power. How did the person involved with creating the world react? He met each temptation by quoting relevant scripture, like Cherie remembering Proverbs 27:12. This is our second key strategy.

Can we, do we, copy that in our temptations? Do we have enough of God's word embedded in our minds to be specific? For those three areas that Jesus faced in the areas of ego, physical desires, and power, do you know those verses he used? Or others that work for you?

Let's combine my failings with frankness. Regardless of how great your pastor teaches the Bible, 30 to 45 minutes on Sunday cannot encompass all the situations we face. Do we regularly get into God's word on our own?

If we don't, we've really not done all we can to survive when unexpected spiritual temptations arise.

Kick-Starting the Application

How well do you prepare ahead for tough times? How frequently do you, individually, get into God's word? How can you do better?

DAY FIVE

DANGER ZONE: JESUS CALLS US TO RISK ALL

Speed's Way

With the click on the computer button to confirm the ride, the realization hit me that the danger zone lay ahead. I'd never driven a supercar, particularly one with all that power, and Lamborghinis were known for being a bit brutish. I had no clue how to use the paddle shifter on the Lambo—not quite an automatic, so I would have to shift. I could deftly shift with the clutch on my bike, just feeling the time to change gears. But I didn't know the Lambo like that, nor the paddle shifter, which concerned me.

I knew other cars would be on the track, which made me happy—I'd have a chance to pass them, but we could bump, or even collide. I already discovered my reactions had gotten slower, along with processing new information. The high speeds left less time to react, on a course I'd never driven on, with a lot of curves. One approached 160 degrees, right after the straight. Their requirement of a crash helmet gave a clue. The state of California didn't require them on my Honda Accord. And why do they call them *crash* helmets?

Exotics Racing provided insurance with the cost of the ride, so what did they know that we drivers might not? Would the cost of damage we caused be beyond our ability to take care of it? In the orientation, they told us that if we used too much power coming out of a turn that could make the car slide, and if it pulled a 360-degree turn, they had to pull the car in, examine it, and possibly do some repairs. That would end the ride. And yes, I did break the tires loose once coming out of a turn but quickly recovered. Honestly, it was fun.

Yes, all of those dangers could be addressed. I read and watched numerous videos about paddle shifting and about the quirks of driving the Gallardo 550. That's where I learned it wasn't known as a driver's car, like the Porsche GT3. The Lambo models get named after bulls, which gave a clue about them. Exotics provided all of us newbie drivers a good orientation on what to do and what to avoid, then took us out for two laps in a Porsche SUV to demonstrate it.

Then came the ride. Megan, the instructor next to me in the car, kept shouting directions on when to brake, to turn, to accelerate. She kept her eyes behind us for approaching cars so I could focus on what lay ahead. If a car approached me, I would have to slow down and let it pass. She told me when to shift.

But they still required the helmet.

God's Way

Frankly, following Jesus has more of a danger zone. Think about the cost of following Jesus: "For whoever wants to save their life will lose it, but whoever loses their life for me will find it" (Matthew 16:25). Think about the personal change in moving away from the person and behavior we've become comfortable with, as we become a new person: "And we all, who with unveiled faces contemplate the Lord's glory, are being transformed into his image with ever-increasing glory, which comes from the Lord, who is the Spirit" (2 Corinthians 3:18). Yes, a great change, but a soul renovation, Jesus style.

Think about yielding our preferred lifestyle and comforts to serve. Paul had all the advantages he could possess—an educated Jew, respected and admired, in a culture he felt comfortable in—yet left all he knew and had to tell non-Jewish people about Jesus. People today still who leave their countries because God told them go, and they did.

Think about—maybe not so much in America, but around the world—the risk of losing our lives. Jesus: killed. Stephen, an early leader: killed. James, an apostle and brother of John: killed. Apart from Judas, all the apostles were martyred, except John. More followers of Jesus died for their faith in the last century than all the previous combined.

Jesus is called a lion. Good but not safe. Let's not allow the risk to hinder our pursuit of the abundant life, of moving into the danger zone, of more fully growing and serving. Here are two practical steps.

First, focus on God's presence in our lives. Just as I had Megan alongside so I didn't face the dangers alone, so do we have our Lord with us. Always. Listen to God's encouragement to Joshua just before he began the dangerous move into the Promised Land: "Be strong and courageous. Do not be afraid; do not be discouraged, for the Lord your God will be with you wherever you go" (Joshua 1:9).

The more we realize God himself accompanies us, the more strength and courage we have to handle the hard times that often come with following him. We don't have to rely on our natural courage or strength, but the Son of God himself rides with us. Every lap.

But let's go further. Just like Megan's presence brought comfort and her expertise helped me drive fast, God works with us: "We know that in everything God works for good with those who love him, who are called according to his purpose" (Romans 8:28 RSV). Like Megan's hand on my shoulder telling me to let the driver behind safely pass, God's hand touches every aspect of our lives. And it works. Like I did with Megan, we just need to follow his instructions.

Crossing the Finish Line

Do you tend to like challenges and risks or stability and safety? How does this Day speak to that? Think of some past challenges in your faith. How did you handle them—with God or a sense of being alone? Did you trust in God to work for good in them? What risks do you face right now or see in the near future? What can you do now to best prepare for them?

DAY SIX

A CHANGING RIDER: ADAPTING RIDING STYLES

Day Eight, "A Changing World," uses changes in our roads as a metaphor for deeper societal issues. Not only do roads change, but riders do too, so let's examine these. For most of our Gray Hog rides, we had a long first day just to reach the main part of our ride. Six hundred fifty miles became typical, sometimes more. I'd usually get up at 4:00 a.m. to avoid the SoCal traffic, and I loved seeing the sunrise off to my right, with the darkness slowly disappearing until the sun burst over the mountains to my east.

The longest ride together came at age 70, when I began one of our long trips to Canada with an Iron Butt ride: 1,080 miles in 16.3 hours to Dillon, Montana. I met Jerry in Butte for breakfast, then we rode 1,100 miles to Duluth to bag more states, before we rode 1,000 miles back to Shelby, Montana, to meet Mick and Brad and head into Canada. So, 3,100 miles before we reached the target. And we loved it! The challenge, the break from the routine of work brought joy. A fine accomplishment.

Then in 2022, at 75 and 74, Jerry and I headed from the West Coast for the East to bag some states and see new territory, so we did the same long days, absolutely necessary to finish the 8,500 miles. But it beat us up. We both made some mistakes in judgment and had to take a day off to rest. Then, after 5,000 miles our bikes failed us, so Jerry flew home and I rented a car.

That marked a tipping point, and our three rides since have changed. Before, rarely did we stay in the same motel two nights in a row—now it's the goal. We'd typically take off around sunrise and ride until 5:00 p.m. or so. Now, we leave later in the morning, arrive mid-afternoon, do an easy sightseeing loop the next day, then journey on the day after. It saves packing, but more so, we have a slow day to see the local country, and our bodies get a chance to rest more than on those earlier rides.

Rarely do we hit 600 miles, and some of our days, even those from one motel to another, range around 200 to 300 miles. Why? Both Jerry and this rider have changed. In our mid-70s, we can't ride like we did in our 20s. Or our 60s. Even our early 70s. But we ride. Yeah, sometimes we'll do the long day, but reluctantly. Usually it's only the first day to get in place, and then we try to stay there two nights. As I write this Day in January 2025, we're talking about a possible long trip in May to Colorado and New Mexico, and all days come in under 400 miles. That used to be a morning ride, like the Iron Butt, reaching Cedar City after 450 miles came at 11:00 a.m. Notice the past tense.

The key: We adapt. Shakespeare encouraged us to be true to our own selves, but we need to acknowledge that we change. Peter experienced that, when Jesus prophesied about him: "Very truly I tell you, when you were younger you dressed yourself and went where you wanted; but when you are old you will stretch out your hands, and someone else will dress you and lead you where you do not want to go" (John 21:18). Age changes us. It seems like my health took a nosedive at 75, and my doctor told me that our cells change significantly at 40 and 70. Well, I extended that five years, but it still arrived. Hence, the shorter rides. I often say I can still do much of what I did at 27 but for not as long, and I pay for it longer.

Yes, we can compensate. We learn how to do things better and easier. We stretch and exercise and stay in shape. We exercise our minds. But like Rod McKuen said long ago, "No clock can stop the coming of time." Peter and I both agree and say, "Amen!"

Our experiences also change us, again like Peter. We first met him as a commercial fisherman with some spiritual interest. Then he became a sold-out but impulsive follower. By the end of his life, he emerged as a wise sage writing two New Testament books filled with grace and advice. I'm intrigued how God has crafted my professional life after leaving college: seven jobs in nine years helped me to identify with all. Then came ministry: four churches in 24 years, which required digging deeper into God and his word. That led to Christian education on the university and secondary levels, with five institutions in 15 years, and that to writing, now 14 books in 31 years, reaching far more people than the years spent in ministry. God walked me through each experience, and each succeeding step only came from the ones before.

Yes, some changes damage us. My novel *Wild Rides* details the bad decisions that many of my family made, that hurt themselves and others. Some chose to remain a victim. Others chose redemption. We choose to become bitter or to learn.

So we adapt. We keep in tune with the changing us. We identify our strengths, our weaknesses, our joys, our talents, our gifts, our personality. We recognize that all people are shaped differently, based on their DNA, family, experiences, and more. Those differences certainly include stages of life.

In all our changes, may we choose to learn and grow.

Kick-Starting the Application

What changes are you experiencing, whether better recognizing your gifts and abilities to areas you don't shine in? As you go through the years, how has your sense of identity refined itself? Are you now working and serving God in your sweet spot, that's made for you? How have your goals changed as you have changed?

DAY SEVEN

THE OLD '69 CAMARO

Murray Pura

Murray lives and writes in southwestern Alberta near to Waterton-Glacier Peace Park (Montana and Alberta). He has been promoted by HarperCollins, Baker, Barbour, Zondervan, and several other publishing houses. Literary honors include the Hemingway Award (CIBA Seattle), the Word Guild Award (Toronto), and the Blue Ridge Selah Literary Award (North Carolina).

Speed's Way

Around 1995, we needed a second vehicle for my wife. I was looking into new cars or pickups. Then a friend said he had an old '69 Camaro RS (Rally Sport).

Ah, 1969. One of the iconic years for American muscle cars. I had no idea what I was getting into, but I got into it anyway. I aligned myself with a body shop and began learning about doors that weighed 100 pounds, paint codes (frost green), 1968 (the tire jack was wrapped in a '68 newspaper), stock parts for a '69 Chevy Camaro, detailing engine blocks, finding fuel that had enough lead in it to ensure the car ran efficiently and effectively.

I read all kinds of books and manuals. Scouted about online. Spent hours on eBay. Learned more not only about Camaros but muscle cars right down the line including Mustang Cobras and Plymouth Barracudas. I remembered how the preacher's kid somehow had a purple Barracuda when we were teens and used to drag race it with me white-knuckling it in the copilot's seat. He never lost a race to anyone.

So over months the old '69 went from battered to beautiful and from drab to vibrant. The engine stopped coughing and hummed instead. One small tap on the gas and the Camaro roared and surged forward like a UFC fighter on an adrenalin rush. People turned to look. During one test drive when she stalled, two biker dudes with hair and beards to the asphalt climbed off their Harleys to help: "Can't leave a car like that lying in the road!"

Renewal and restoration is possible, but it takes time and effort and wisdom. Prayer treated like magic transforms nothing. Prayer for guidance and strength and understanding makes all the difference.

I always liked the Beauty and the Beast fable because the Beast himself was transformed into Beauty. Not just the young woman who beautiful at the end; the beast became it too.

Just as the car went from rust and broken door hinges and an ill-tuned engine in a body without color to as good as new, we can also go from less, depleted, depressed, and unmotivated to more. Much, much more under the strong and skillful workers' hands of God.

The frost green was a Christmas surprise for my wife. (Green is her favorite color, it so happens.) She received no gifts, just a key. Yet that small key was everything—it opened the door and ignited the power. Soon the neighbors had the window-rattling experience (literally) of a rejuvenated muscle car back on the roads of another century.

This is a metaphor for us. Back on the roads in another century, at another age, in a different life. Made new by him who makes all things new.

In the midst of death and destruction and a depleted and diminished spirit by Jeremiah, God told him, "The steadfast love of the Lord never ceases; his mercies never come to an end; they are new every morning; great is your faithfulness" (Lamentations 3:22–23).

DAY SEVEN

God's Way

That love and mercy restore us. Those who grew up in a world of heroes and optimism in the early to mid-1960s (yeah, the Camaro and Mustang era) focused on the good, rarely revealing our flaws. We had to at least seem heroic. Our society has become more willing to acknowledge our flaws; we need restoration.

Our neediness prompted Jesus's incarnation and resurrection, which allow us to approach him. Compare that to Murray swapping some cash for the pink slip of that Camaro. What a waste if he had just parked it in the garage and left it like that. But Murray loved the car as it was and also too much to leave like that.

The Camaro's restoration began when Murray got the pink and started the process. God does the same. Out of mercy, he wants to bring out our best.

We call coming to Christ a fresh start, a new beginning. But it goes much deeper: "This means that anyone who belongs to Christ has *become a new person.* The old life is gone; a new life has begun!" (2 Corinthians 5:17 NLT). This where the metaphor ends: The Camaro remained a Camaro—no transformation into a Shelby GT500.

Ponder that significance. Our unique soul continues, but this change touches our entire being. Every fiber. First, our identity changes, to be a Christ-one, a follower. The rate of our spiritual progress is determined by how much and how soon we understand this new identity and incorporate it into our lives.

Once we do that, the restoration process begins: "You have taken off your old self with its practices and have put on the new self, which is *being renewed* in knowledge in the image of its Creator. Here there is no Greek or Jew, circumcised or uncircumcised, barbarian, Scythian, slave, or free, but *Christ is all and is in all*" (Colossians 3:9–11 BSB).

Let me geek out on the Greek verb *being renewed.* Its present tense indicates now and continuing. The active voice means we do something. And the singular applies it to each individual. Together, they result in no divisions between followers, regardless of their different colors or politics. To the extent that we build walls, we slow down our restoration.

What keeps the restoration process going? Letting Jesus be our all, in all. Or we live out the Christ life, and he changes us in a process. A writing friend, Woody Woodburn, author of *The Butterfly Tree*, posted this on Facebook: "The legendary cellist Pablo Casals was asked why he continued to practice at age 90. 'Because I think I'm making progress.'"

Our question: Do we continue to progress in our restoration?

The Finishing Line

How much have you integrated the concept of being a new person into your walk with Jesus? What impact has that answer had? What is the most significant spiritual change in your last two years? What does that suggest?

DAY EIGHT

A CHANGING WORLD: REACTING TO OUTSIDE CHANGES

Nearing the end of our 2024 ride to Idaho, Jerry and I split off in John Day, Oregon, where Highways 395 and 26 met. He went west on 26 as I turned south on my beloved 395, both riding home solo, an enjoyable part of our trips. It seems like the best trips include that combination, at least for this introvert. Jerry claims to be one as well, but I have my doubts about him, as he does about me.

I spent my last solo night farther south in the Owens Valley town of Lone Pine, then pulled out from the motel at 7:00 a.m., hoping to get the 240 miles home to Temecula before the traffic congealed into an unholy mess. I've discovered the LA to San Bernardino basins become parking lots around 2:00 p.m., so riding schedules have to deal with that. Traffic and bikes don't make particularly pleasing partners.

Not long after departing, a road sign announced a welcomed passing lane ahead, which alleviated my concerns about some slow trucks clogging the single lane. But the promised passing lane soon proved to be closed for construction, with no alternative in sight. Perplexed, I looked around and off in the distance to my right spotted heavy construction, just north of the very small town called Olancha.

DAY EIGHT

Turns out Cal Trans had decided to change the route to bypass the entire Olancha area, and it looks like they're building a pretty wide road off to the west.

I guess that will help the traffic flow, which is nice, but will likely kill the remaining business there. The Rancho House Café was a regular stop for Dad and me, and we'd get gas at the rock-walled Union Gas Station with a red Coca-Cola cooler outside the door. Well, both had been closed for years, but I enjoyed the memories that seeing them provided.

Getting closer to home revealed more road changes, often a four-lane freeway, quite a contrast to the washboard dirt road Dad took to Rock Creek starting in 1925. And ticky-tack homes now crowd together shoulder to shoulder where once only the desert thrived. Add on every fast food or shop that covers America to the mess. The formerly empty desert has changed into a small metropolis. Cheaper housing draws more people. And traffic.

Fortunately, that first road had changed; what took Dad an entire day could now be done leisurely in six hours. Dad would point out the old roads to me along the way. With the changing of the guard, I've taken that responsibility of pointing out the old roads to my grandson and friends. I suspect they're not as thrilled as I had been—the past intrigues me. Frankly, this overall change makes me uneasy. Yes, the travel will improve, allowing more people to trek north and fill the campgrounds and clutter the streams. No, Cal Trans didn't consult me.

Nor did a changing culture. But in spite of that insult, I've chosen to accept both of these changes as reality. I doubt I can change the plans of Cal Trans or the slant of society; my meager voice won't suffice. Honestly, I'll likely not take the bypass into Olancha more than once to see the change; I will bypass my past in the interest of getting to my stream sooner. Much more significantly, I still desire to have some influence on our culture. Surveys indicate that most Americans are uneasy about many of the changes, so we may have a fertile field to sow seeds in.

But to do that means recognizing the changes, not complaining about them. Too much.

We choose to complain or adapt. I opt for the latter. Because as culture changes, we need to know it enough to speak to people where they are. Not to agree but to understand, to listen, to get them. Why do they make their decisions? What are their values? What motivates them? Those answers must come from them, not our assumptions about them. If we assume we can apply our values to them, we'll find it difficult to understand one another.

As a result, too often Christianity is viewed as judgmental and controlling. Too many see our passion as hatred. And we cannot connect. So what do we do?

We speak God's unchanging truth in love. I appreciate 1 Chronicles 12:32 (NLT): "From the tribe of Issachar . . . these men *understood the signs of the times* and knew the best course for Israel to take." Their choices came from knowledge of the times. The culture. The changes.

Responding to the times. Paul did that, crafting his delivery to match his audience, whether Jewish or Greek. Paul knew his audiences and how to reach each: "To the Jews I became like a Jew, to win the Jews. To those under the law I became like one under the law (though I myself am not under the law), so as to win those under the law.[21] To those not having the law I became like one not having the law (though I am not free from God's law but am under Christ's law), so as to win those not having the law.[22] To the weak I became weak, to win the weak. I have become all things to all people so that by all possible means I might save some.[23] I do all this for the sake of the gospel" (1 Corinthians 9:20–23).

He never compromised on the gospel, merely how he presented it to different groups, with different values, with different world views. He knew and quoted their literature. He responded to their idols without judgment, using them as a launch point to introduce Jesus. And always, he demonstrated love.

May we do that same in our changing world.

DAY EIGHT

Kick Starting the Application

Do you keep track of the cultural and moral changes occurring today? Do you have a variety of news sources to gain a more balanced view of those you don't agree with? Do you tend to complain or adjust to cultural changes? What causes that? Can those on the changed side sense your love of them or your disapproval? How can you stay true to God's standards amid changing values?

DAY NINE

A SYMPHONY OF THE SENSES: THE DANGERS OF TECH

Michael Scott

Michael is professor emeritus at California State University, Chico, where he taught in the School of Communication and Education. He also is a former instructor for Hooked On Driving and a former National Auto Sport Association license holder.

Speed's Way

My first experience on a motorcycle had me perched atop the maroon tank of my dad's 1950 Triumph, my short, chubby legs held snug between his Levi's-covered thighs and knees—my small torso safely tucked inside his zippered leather jacket. I was four years old. My dad was twenty-two, confident in his ability to keep us safe and certain that I would get just as much of a thrill out of the experience as he did. He was right on both counts.

Sports vehicles provide a feast for the senses. As my dad knew, that experience must be lived to be fully understood. You have to *ride* a motorcycle to appreciate why nearly nine million Americans have a license to do just that. Some use their bikes to commute, some join clubs devoted to a specific brand, while others push their limits off-road or carve through the sweeping curves of a highway like the Anza-Borrego.

Talk to them and they'll likely tell you these vehicles aren't just a physical act. On the right day, in the right place, they can be a spiritual experience.

Of course, you don't need a vehicle to feel that deep connection between the physical world and the spiritual. I've experienced it on a remote hiking trail, surrounded by the beauty of creation; on a deserted ski run, listening to the hush of the snow; and at full speed in an open-cockpit sports car, my senses firing in concert as I braked hard before a turn. While the method of movement may change, one thing remains constant: In those moments, my senses were in direct contact with the real world. The warmth of the sun on my face, the stillness in the air, and the pull of gravity shifting as I braked—these were proof of something deeper.

Yet I regularly see people trade these vivid, sensory experiences for something far less fulfilling. The modern world encourages us to live through screens—scrolling endlessly, losing hours to digital games that simulate adventure while we remain motionless. Social media tempts us with curated versions of life, offering the illusion of connection while keeping us detached from the tangible world around us. We spend more time capturing moments for others to see than actually living them.

In doing so, we dull our senses. The wind in our faces, the fresh scent of the earth after a storm, the way our muscles tense and relax with movement—these are things no screen can replicate. The more we retreat into the digital, the more we deprive ourselves of what makes life visceral and real. Unlike the passive nature of technology, experiences like riding, hiking, skiing, or simply feeling the ground beneath our feet remind us that we are part of something greater. They wake us up. They sharpen our senses instead of numbing them. And they offer something a screen never can—a true sense of presence in the world, in creation itself.

Our challenge is to reclaim what we've lost—not by rejecting technology entirely but by choosing to engage more fully with the world beyond it. We need to seek out experiences that demand our presence, that force us to feel, to move, to connect in ways that no algorithm can replicate. Whether it's the rush of a motorcycle leaning into a turn, clipping the apex of a curve in your sports car, the quiet solitude of a mountain trail, or the simple act of looking someone in the eye instead of at a screen, these moments remind us what it means to be alive. They reconnect us to the real, to creation, to ourselves.

God's Way

At each step of creation, God proclaimed its goodness, culminating in the arrival of humans, to whom he gave his world to manage, to use and enjoy. I suspect sports car drivers and bikers have a special affinity for it: we're not encompassed in a cage of steel, but in the midst of it, experiencing it directly. Mike gets that, encouraging us to wisely decrease whatever disconnects us from it. Steel cages or some technologies.

In one draft he wrote, "Reality is to be lived, all five senses working in concert and in contact with the physical world. When we fail to use them routinely and as intended, I believe, they soon dull to the majesty of the world around us." In revising, he took it out, but these words wisely challenge us to review our lifestyles and practices: Are we taking full advantage of this marvelous world? I had to put these wise words back in.

How often do we share a magnificent photo of nature, with the qualifier, "This can't begin to show all of the beauty, but . . ."? We recognize the primacy of directly experiencing the world. An early poem of mine, not too long after my first ride from SoCal to Canada, caught that.

DAY NINE

Glory in nature
in each part
    of the world about you
see the symmetry of a cedar
    stretching to the skies
feel the rough graininess of sand
    between fingers
and the softness of rabbit's fur
    on your cheek
breathe deeply of piney mountain air
    as it searches out your lungs
count the timeless
    ocean's crests
Yes
    glory in each part
    of the earth
        from which you came
    treasure it
    use it
and hear it gently shout
    from where you got your breath

Ponder these passages of the senses God gave us:

"How sweet are your words to my *taste*. How sweet are your words to my taste!" (Psalm 119:103).

"Look at my hands and my feet. It is I myself! *Touch* me and see" (Luke 24:39).

"Walk in the way of love, just as Christ loved us and gave himself up for us as a *fragrant* offering" (Ephesians 5:2).

"*Hear*, O Israel: The Lord our God, the Lord is one" (Deuteronomy 6:4).

Whether with a sports car or bike, a walk through the neighborhood or sky diving, sense the world, and its creator.

Crossing the Finish Line

Have you often connected fully using your senses to better connect with God? Which sense, for you, does that best?

DAY TEN

ANTICIPATE THE BLESSINGS: PARALYZED BY ANTICIPATED PROBLEMS?

Toby Erickson

Toby resides with his wife near their grandchildren in eastern Washington. When not riding, he makes regular moto-camping tours to stay connected with his California family and enjoys woodworking, teaching Sunday school, and writing. He has also written Raise Your Own Dang Kids.

Before a trip, the kind of problems that may await me grabs my attention more than the blessings God may bring.

When starting out on a road trip on my Suzuki DL-1000 V-STROM Adventure Bike, I look over my scooter, service everything, kick the tires, pack everything I need, check the GPS for issues along the route, look at the weather app, and prepare for the worst.

For my journey through the Pacific Northwest, I broke it into legs with different landscapes and people to see along the route. This zig-zag route would bring me through mountains, coastal views, deserts, high passes, and small towns.

But as I started out on this 10-day trip, the joy robber worry got into my head: "What is that weird noise? Did I remember to pack my special pillow? Is there going to be road construction on 97? And what is that weird noise?"

On the leg between Sisters and Newport, Oregon, on the coast, that nagging sound started to get louder. It had to be some kind of vibration in the wheel bearing or drive train. Pulling into a trailhead parking lot along the Santiam Pass, I broke out my tools to work on the noise. My chain seemed loose, which was puzzling because that was something I had attended to before leaving home in Spokane. Tightening a chain is pretty straightforward, so I did that.

The noise persisted. Images of the chain dropping off seizing up on a tight curve, or worse, started persisting in my mind. What could I do about it with no one around and no cell service? Each curve had me wincing, clenching my teeth, and feeling vulnerable to the possibility of a life-altering incident. Should I stop and admit defeat? This beautiful stretch of road brought no joy.

Before long, the road straightened out as I entered Sweet Home, Oregon. My hopes rose when I saw a mechanic shop.

There stood Kyle, the owner and sole mechanic at the shop—young, spry, kind of quiet, and yet totally equipped to get me on my way. He dropped down onto the blacktop and started spinning and yanking on all things drivetrain. As I shared with him my plans to get all the way to Markleeville and back again to Spokane, Kyle assured me I would only need a new chain . . . and he had one. With great skill and a meticulous manner, Kyle zipped off my old chain, slickly drawing a new chain through the inner sprocket without requiring further disassembly. Within 30 minutes, that old Suzuki was as good as new. Kyle didn't charge me nearly what his service deserved, so I tipped him a bit, and I got back on my way, praises reverberating in my helmet as I went!

The solace I so look forward to on a road trip as that black ribbon rolls on often becomes a nagging cacophony of doubt, fear, and angst.

Then I try to remember who God is, who I am in him, and why he calls me out on the road in the first place. Of course, problems and unknowns accompany the ride, but the wonder and beauty of it all shows how God comes through. I want to anticipate that!

We humans tend to look ahead. Optimists expect a good future. Pessimists expect the worst. Truthfully, we don't really know what will happen; only God possesses omniscience. But when we expect bad to come, we invite that joy robber of worry into our souls. Before the trip, Toby did what he could, but then worry invaded, which decreased the pleasure of the ride. And when the problem arose, his worry magnified it until he pondered it causing a "life-altering moment."

But C. S. Lewis gave a deeper spiritual result of worry in *The Screwtape Letters*, as a demon gave this advice on how to separate Jesus followers from God: "There is nothing like suspense and anxiety for barricading a human's mind against the Enemy. He wants men to be concerned with what they do; our business is to keep them thinking about what will happen to them."

Perhaps that explains why Jesus condemned worry in the Sermon on the Mount in Matthew 6:25–34. Those 10 verses used *worry* six times. Here are some selected verses, but you might read the larger passage on your own.

> "So do not *worry*, saying, 'What shall we eat?' or 'What shall we drink?' or 'What shall we wear?' For the pagans run after all these things, and your heavenly Father knows that you need them. But seek first his kingdom and his righteousness, and all these things will be given to you as well. Therefore, do not *worry* about tomorrow, for tomorrow will *worry* about itself. Each day has enough *trouble* of its own."

Notice that last line, that each day has its troubles, so we deal with the issues of the day, like Toby did. We don't ignore reality; we don't minimize genuine threats or issues. We respond to them to the best of our ability, but we don't borrow unreal future problems and bring them into our present.

Long ago a wise friend suggested we worry about two things: those we can do something about and those we can do nothing about. So if we can do something, we do it. If we can't do anything, why worry?

Jesus asked what we run after: the stuff of life, or the Creator of life? Then he promised that when we put God first as Lord, we can trust him be with us and strengthen us in the worst of times. Worry about what *might* happen reveals a lack of trust in God, a lack of running after him. Choosing to avoid worry allows us to anticipate the blessings God brings.

Kick Starting the Application

Do you lean toward optimism or pessimism? What has caused that? Have you thought before of worry as a lack of trust in God? When you start to worry, can you create a phrase to get your focus on God, not the worry?

DAY ELEVEN

TRUST THE INSTRUCTOR: SHE KNEW BETTER THAN I

Speed's Way

My love for speed came early and honestly. Growing up, I frequently heard Dad telling how he and a friend officially broke the Cannonball Run record in 1929, driving from New York City to the Santa Monica pier in a Ford Model A roadster, covering 3,364 miles in 77 hours and 2 minutes. I have the newspaper article and pics. Some roads were washboard dirt, and once a cop stopped them.

Then on a family trip from SoCal to Utah when I was eight, Dad pushed his 55 Ford Fairlane 500 V8 up to 120 in the Nevada desert, kept it between 105 and 115 for 100 miles, and it hooked me. (Okay, he ran out of gas seven miles before Ely, Nevada.) I've driven fast—a lot—and have driven several nice cars, a Nissan Z, Corvettes, even a race-bred Lotus Elan. And when I lived in the mountains above Taos with a full-sized Ford van, only a Z passed me. Once. I could corner decently, and speed didn't intimidate me.

But I knew the Lamborghini at Exotics Racing far transcended anything I knew, so I listened to the pre-ride briefing and to the onboard instructor Megan's orientation about the strengths and quirks of the Gallardo. You could stall it off the line. The brakes caught unexpectedly quickly. Her advice on accelerating and braking and cornering were new, though.

Accelerate until you see the two cones near the start of the turn, then brake. At the single green cone quit braking, hit the gas some, and turn toward the apex as straight as you can. Once passing it, gently accelerate until you see the next green cone, point it straight, then floor it. I tried. This actually makes the turn slightly longer than hugging the inside, but you get through it more quickly.

But consistently I took my foot off the gas before the cones and turned in too soon. That worked well with my earlier vehicles but not the Gallardo. My earlier habits of fast turns took time to get over. And once on exiting the turn, I hit the gas too hard and too soon, and the rear tires broke free a bit. Kind of fun, but it slows you down.

Megan soon shouted, "Not yet!" when I started to coast; "Not yet!" again as I turned in too soon; and "Now!" as we exited a turn. Finally, her words overcame my previous habits. I did it right, screamed around the corner, tires screeching, and shot like a rocket out of the turn. On my first lap, a slow "get to know the car and course" lap, another Lambo had passed me. Now I returned the favor and passed him after leaving a turn. On a short straight that led to a 170-degree turn, my Lambo hit 112.

We seemed to be in synch as I seamlessly moved from curve to straight and back into a curve. I learned I could trust what Megan said. It worked.

God's Way

When we claim the name of Christian, many of us follow him through the twists of life like I did, before my Lambo lessons. We have our actions, ones that work decently. We have a culture, one we desire to fit into. We have family, with their teachings and expectations. We have our desires; we want to live our lives as we want, when and how. We have our experiences, that have taught us how to get by, that became embedded habits. We listen, but we follow like my first Lambo laps. Missing a lot of the Lambo potential.

Too soon. Too late. Too slow. Too fast. Incorrectly. We all possess flaws. We have weaknesses. Blind spots. We think we know better than others. So we approach life as I approached driving the Lambo: ignorant of so much. We make mistakes as children that affect our adult lives. Adult mistakes compound the problems.

Too often we view God as an adviser, one who suggests options that we can choose or reject. But we're in the driver's seat. Besides, so much of his advice seems ancient, made for other people in other times. So we try to drive a Lambo like our Honda Accord, and we don't really experience what a Lambo can do.

We miss the best from God. Why? We don't fully trust our instructor. I quickly realized Megan knew far more than I about letting the Lambo be a Lambo. Following her instructions changed how I drove. Following God's instructions will change how we follow him.

Paul battled that same tendency: "I have discovered this principle of life—that when I want to do what is right, I inevitably do what is wrong. . . . Oh, what a miserable person I am! Who will free me from this life that is dominated by sin and death? Thank God! The answer is in Jesus Christ our Lord" (Romans 7:21, 24–25 NLT). Sounds like my early laps.

Here's why we can trust him—he made it all and best knows how life functions. Here's a simple verse with huge implications, "In the beginning God created the heavens and the earth" (Genesis 1:1). So we listen to our spiritual instructor. We follow his leading, his commands. We strive to know him more intimately, continually.

After our briefing, I watched Megan and the other instructors hop in the cars to warm them up. They screamed around the track at speeds beyond my imagination. I saw her do it, and that helped me trust her commands. That trust enabled me to scream a bit too.

Crossing the Finishing Line

Brutally think about your life. How much do you trust that God truly knows best? Don't focus on what you know should be true, but what would your actions reveal? When you go against him, what primary reasons do you have? In practical terms, what can you do to develop more trust in God as your instructor in racing through life?

DAY TWELVE

RIDE RELAXED

After our 2023 ride, Jerry thought the time had arrived to hang up his biker boots. So for 2024, Rich and I planned a tour to Colorado and Taos, New Mexico, my beloved former home. Rich, who lives in South Dakota, and I met in Taos earlier for a ride, and he fell in love with Taos. But as they say, "Man proposes and God disposes," and some issues arose that required Rich to bail out, so it looked like my first long solo ride in some time.

Then Jerry's Goldwing couldn't sell, his back got better, and he proposed an option. We could meet in Ogden, Utah, then head into the mountains of central Idaho. That would be much shorter and more doable than Colorado and New Mexico, and I'd rather ride with Jerry than alone.

We planned to meet in Ogden on Sunday, May 19, 2024, so the day before, at 7:00 a.m., I pulled out of Temecula on I-15 heading north with reservations in Richfield, Utah, about 560 miles away. An easy jaunt for my Honda CTX1300 and doable on the 76-year-old body. A brief gas stop in Barstow led to lunch in Vegas at a decent sandwich shop next to the gas station. Double dipping, I guess. Then a lot of deserts until I passed St. George at 400 miles, with just over two hours to go. But after Cedar City the clouds began rolling in, some white, some pretty dark. With some I could see the rain slapping the ground ahead, then the road turned away for 10 miles, and I thought I dodged the storm.

But few roads near the Utah mountains stay straight, and the next turn took me right into the darkest clouds, and the rain came down. Hard. With no place to get off and needing to make it to Richfield, that gave me no choice except to go on. I flashed back 10 years to a trip to meet the guys in Rexburg, Idaho. Our destination: Glacier National Park. The same road, the same spot, not much past Cedar, and that storm brought heavy enough winds that I had to lean the bike left to offset the west winds, and I hunkered down in my jacket and behind the windscreen. Not much help, and I tightened my grip to keep control of the bike in the storm for over 40 miles. My lower back and my trapezius muscles below my neck felt like iron, and the hot tub at the Nephi motel soothed me for well over an hour before my muscles loosened.

But I learned a lesson: When it gets cold or windy or wet, relax. That sounds counterintuitive, but it works. So when this rain came down, I told my body to let go a little, to not tighten up. Yeah, that may require repeated and out-loud communication. When Richfield arrived, the old body felt pretty decent. Maybe not good, but decent is okay.

I responded on the first storm like most of us do when hard times and problems and worries hit us. We tighten up. We grip stronger. But perhaps the lesson learned on the first trip and applied on the second also applies to following Jesus. When we face difficulties, maybe we should counterintuitively chill. Relax in the face of our rain. Don't expect the rain to stop, but just go to God. Yes, that sounds easy, so let's explore it and make it practical.

One verse has saved my sanity multiple times: "Don't worry about anything; instead, pray about everything. Tell God what you need, and thank him for all he has done. *Then* you will experience God's peace, which exceeds anything we can understand" (Philippians 4:6–7, NLT). Some time back I learned that we can worry about two categories: some we can do something about, some we can do nothing about. If we can do something, we don't worry; just do what we can do. If we can't do anything, why worry about it?

Notice the transition in that passage: Don't worry, pray instead; *then* you'll get God's peace. Kind of an oxymoron to worry when having God's peace, right? Years back a guy in our college career group gave us a plaque that said, "Sometimes the Lord calms the storm. Sometimes he lets the storm rage, and calms his child." Let me suggest we choose to let God calm us when we refuse to worry about it. When we refuse to grip tight enough to maintain control of the situation. Gripping too strong may keep God from doing his stuff.

In researching for today, I found a new insight on a very familiar verse, "Be still, and know that I am God." But I discovered that the context significantly affects the meaning. "Come and see what the Lord has done, the desolations he has brought on the earth. He makes wars cease to the ends of the earth. He breaks the bow and shatters the spear; he burns the shields with fire. He says, 'Be still, and know that I am God; I will be exalted among the nations, I will be exalted in the earth'" (Psalm 46:8–10).

The context shows God acting in the world, then the command to be still. Relax. Don't take it all on yourself. Get out of his way. We interfere with God working in our lives when we grip too tight. Of course, we find a balance. Letting go of the handlebars would have insured a crash. Hanging on too tight racked my body.

Maybe when trials arrive, we can pray, "God, please stop the storm, but most importantly, may I avoid worry by resting in you. You've got me, whatever happens." That presence can bring us a relaxing calm. Trusting his ability to work in all things kills worry and stress.

Kick-Starting the Application

Do you sometimes fight your obstacles and concerns by stressing, by pulling into yourself? How much worry do you carry? Have you tried praying about everything and thanking God for his presence and peace? Will you do that with your next hard time?

DAY THIRTEEN

STEPPING UP IN A SPORTS CAR: BALANCING WANT AND NEED

Jim Davis

Jim Davis is a retired history and photography teacher. Besides cars in general, his interests include fishing, traveling, and playing with the worship band at his local church. He also contributed to Tim's devotional, More God, Motorcycles, and the Open Road. *He lives with his wife of over 44 years, Crystal, in Murrieta, California.*

Speed's Way

For the past 20 years, we have owned a convertible. At the same time, we have also owned at least two other vehicles. Since 2001, one pulls our travel trailer. From 2001 to 2013, a Chevrolet Tahoe did that. When it got to the point of needing some extensive repairs, we traded it in for a Dodge Ram diesel truck.

Along with that, we have also possessed a SUV for use on fishing trips where the truck could not easily go. Currently, our Lexus GX470 is our long-distance vehicle for its very smooth ride.

But for many years, we had dreamed of a Mustang convertible. Why? For the obvious reasons—they're fun and sexy. Not necessarily a status symbol, since they are relatively inexpensive, especially used.

DAY THIRTEEN

In 2003, our dreams finally came true. Our boys had made us empty nesters, so we bought a 2002 Mustang, with metallic red paint, a black top, and a leather interior. For you gearheads, no, it was not a GT. My wife, with her fibromyalgia, could not find a comfortable seating position in the seats of the GT. But ours met the long-term desire for a Mustang.

We enjoyed it for 17 years, primarily as my wife's commuter. But it also took a couple of top-down trips to Las Vegas, and I drove it at Auto Club Speedway on one of their track days—at 100 miles per hour. But approaching 150,000 miles, its age started to show. The paint faded while baking in the sun, the front seats were torn, and about a quart of oil got burned every 500 miles. To fix those things would cost more than the car's worth—time to get something else.

I had decided against another Mustang for several reasons. The GT version was too loud and Ford stopped making the V6 version in 2016. And frankly, I didn't trust the turbocharged four-cylinder motor. Besides, I wanted something with a little more glitz. Was that lust or pride? Maybe pride. After all, we both were retired by then. I was nearing 70, and I guess I wanted to show the world that I had made it.

But if not a Mustang, then what? Several options arose. Camaro? Not much different than a Mustang. Mercedes, BMW, Jaguar? Too expensive and horrible repair and maintenance costs. Chrysler? You're kidding! Volvo? Nope, a hardtop convertible that folds into the trunk. Say goodbye to luggage space.

Then I came across the Audi A5 Cabriolet. Very sleek, elegant, excellent handling, a decent sized trunk, and a very capable turbo-4—and not ridiculously priced. So we bought one, even though it waited 1,000 miles away.

A want? A need? Both? Neither?

Both, and more.

The convertible gives us something the other two vehicles we have cannot do. Escape. When we are in a particularly stressful period, one cannot express the level of joy or relief of driving on the road with some gentle curves, with the top down on a full-moon night. All of our cares go away. It's almost spiritual.

God's Way

Jim and Crystal's sports car saga brings up an issue all humans face: How do we improve our life situation? We're told contentment is good: "I have learned to *be content* whatever the circumstances" (Philippians 4:11). But we're also told to improve our conditions if we can: "Were you a slave when you were called? Don't let it trouble you—although if you can gain your freedom, *do so*" (1 Corinthians 7:21).

Let's examine some tips on how to evaluate need, want, lust, and pride, to help us avoid the extremes of legalism or license, of asceticism or greed. Frankly, I won't tell you what to do, just offering some biblical principles to help navigate this.

Paul addressed eating meat offered to idols, saying it has nothing inherently wrong, but he used a principle that touches this topic today: "But if someone believes it is wrong, then for *that person* it is wrong" (Romans 14:14 NLT). An act that God views as acceptable can be unacceptable if it violates our own conscience and values. The application here?

We shouldn't violate our own conscience on nonbiblical items. This doesn't mean others must follow our conscience; rather, we don't judge others based on our individual conscience. Let's not violate what we individually see as wrong. Maybe we need to study more and adjust our conscience. For me, just for me, as much as I love Lamborghinis, I would feel wrong owning one. If I could afford it, the difference between that Lambo and my Honda could help God's kingdom and the needy. But that only applies to me, not to thee. But if you can afford and own a Lambo, enjoy it! Maybe loan it to me for a day?

We also need to look at our motives. As Jim wrote, was it lust or pride or need or want? Do we use our vehicles as a sense of pride and self-worth? Do we compare our worth to others by the car we drive? Jesus's brother James touched on that: "But if you harbor bitter envy and *selfish ambition* in your hearts, *do not boast* about it or deny the truth" (James 3:14). Anything we do out of selfish ambition that enables us to boast or compare ourselves to others hurts our spiritual depth.

A third tip deals with pragmatism, examining reasons for and against, costs and benefits, particularly in tune with our faith. Our emotions and optimism and desires need the balance of practicality. I mentioned owning a Lambo earlier, and frankly, the purchase and upkeep exceed our resources. Jesus gave some good advice: "Suppose one of you wants to build a tower. Won't you first sit down and estimate the cost to see if you have enough money to complete it?" (Luke 14:28).

Notice how Jim and Crystal factored these into their love of convertibles.

Crossing the Finish Line

Do you have a process on how to make decisions regarding need and want? Do you have any new thoughts from this Day? How does your faith drive decisions?

DAY FOURTEEN

WHEN HOPES GET DASHED

Funny how tastes can vary between long-term friends. In our Gray Hogs group, Mick and I kept eagle eyes out for Dairy Queens, a break to enjoy Blizzards. I'm hooked on chocolate chip cookie dough, and Mick went for variety. Brad grabbed one for sociability, but Jerry didn't care much. But whenever Jerry spotted a Long John Silvers, that would be our lunch or dinner spot. He loves their fish, and even asks for the deep-fried crumbs. Go figure.

Maybe that's why Jerry's hopes got so high on our 2022 East Coast ride. There aren't many of his favorite fish and chip places in the Rockies and Kansas, and on our third day, he spotted one in Hays, Kansas, when we got off for gas and grub. But the context counts. We'd been riding hard; I left Temecula on Friday May 13. When you read Day 40, you'll understand how this suggested an omen.

Day one for me saw 625 miles from Temecula to Salina, Utah, then another 110 to where we met mid-morning in Green River, Utah. Jerry had put on 630 from Keizer, Oregon, to Burley, Idaho, then he rode another 360 to Green River. Limon, Colorado, our next night, lay another 300 miles from Green River.

Getting to Hays totaled 1,565 miles in 2½ days, averaging 625 miles for guys in their mid-70s. Some hard riding, with another 240 before Wichita, our temporary home for the night. At that point, we needed good meals, a hot spa, and firm beds.

So when Jerry saw the Long Johns in Hays, he rejoiced and I grieved, hoping for something better. But our emotions shifted when we discovered this high-class eatery only had a drive-through—no walk-up and no inside seating. Juggling food and drinks on a bike just doesn't work.

Honestly, you should have seen the waves of grief wash across his face. Days of hard riding, thinking he had a LJS reward, only for those hopes to be shattered. I did feel sorry for him, even though it worked out for me.

Then we randomly found a Whiskey Creek restaurant close by, with one of the best brisket sandwiches I've ever tasted. A nice Hazy IPA from a local brewmaster came along, and Jerry had his usual four diet colas, and we stretched out on the comfortably cushioned seats at our booth. A nice break from the road.

I appreciated that brief time in Hays; Sheila and my nephews and nieces attended college at Hays State, but the time came to hop back on the bikes and head for Wichita. My sister-in-law lives there, and my grandfather worked for a local company, putting on music and drama shows to peddle snake oil for the Sa-Tan-Ic Medicine Company. Honest. But that's a story for another book, with a working title of *Choices*.

Hope gives . . . well, hope. The chance of a better future. Looking ahead with a smile, like Jerry when he saw Long John Silver's. Merriam Webster defines the concept as "to cherish a desire with anticipation." The poet Alexander Pope has a famous line: "Hope springs eternal in the human breast: Man never is, but always to be blest."

I suspect God placed hope in our nature to help us visualize better days ahead. Progress. A willingness to keep forging ahead. Hope seems to come naturally to us humans. But hope presents a problem—what Jerry experienced. Hopes can get shattered. They can prove to not be a blessing. Yet despite Jerry's disappointment, the shattered hope didn't devastate him. Why? He realized a hope is just a wish.

DAY FOURTEEN

Merriam Webster continues its definition: "hope implies *little certainty* but suggests . . . the possibility." Long ago I penned a simplistic poem, "Don't allow hope to grow / into expectation / that merely breeds disappointment." Pope said it better: "Blessed is the man who *expects nothing*, for he shall never be disappointed."

When hopes don't come true, we regret that. But when we expect something, the unfilled certainty can bring greater disappointment, pessimism, and a sense of defeat. So maybe we need to strike a balance in our hopes. Our optimistic side hopes for it; our pessimistic side puts on the brakes enough to keep hopes from growing into expectation.

So how do we navigate hopes and expectations?

For our own hopes, simply hold them with a loose grip. Nice if they come true, okay if they don't. Fight the urge to expect them to happen. I've found expecting less results in less disappointment.

How about the hopes in what others say? The same process.

One good friend on a phone call will often say, "Got an important call from my doctor. Let me get that and I'll call you back." Do I hope he does? Of course. But I've learned to not expect a callback, maybe 1 in 50. I just smile and go on. Flawed people will disappoint us, but may they disappoint hopes, not expectations.

One hope we can always allow to grow into expectation: the promises of God, "My soul, wait silently for God alone, *for my expectation is from Him*" (Psalm 62:5 NKJV). Let's not expect him to do what he hasn't promised. Do we expect God provides a raise at work? Better not, since he never promised it. When we expect it, we breed disappointment in God not doing what we expected.

But . . . Expecting God to come through on his promises gives us a bedrock assurance: "it is impossible for God to lie, we who have fled to take hold of the hope set before us may be greatly encouraged. We have *this hope as an anchor for the soul, firm and secure*." (Hebrews 6:18–19). In our changing world, it helps to know some expectations can be trusted.

Yes, we hope. But may our expectations rest in Him.

DAY FOURTEEN

Kick-Starting the Application

Have you felt God disappointed you for not doing what you hoped for? What is a promise from him? How well do you balance hopes and expectations? How much do you trust in God?

DAY FIFTEEN

TRUST THE CAR

Speed's Way

If you desire to see a unique outdoor car museum, come by my house sometime. A few blocks away is a mélange of around 20 cars: four in the driveway, four on the front lawn where they made a second driveway, about six parked on the street in front of the house, and close to another dozen parked by the neighbors' houses.

Don't assume they're Okies with a dirt lawn and a bunch of junker cars. The tasteful landscape and all the cars impress me—some amaze me. A beautiful custom '63 Chevy Impala lowrider, a sweet '56 Chevy Bel Air, 2 *very* nice new Corvettes, several nice new pickups, and more. All nice. All rarely ridden. I've been tempted to stop by and offer to take one off their hands, without charging them much for it.

Seeing all these cars caused me to think back on some of mine and the lessons they gave me.

I learned on a land rocket, a '63 Viking Blue Ford Galaxie 500, with a high-compression V8. My own first car: a '64 Ford Falcon Futura, a Mustang with a different body, looked sporty but the slant 6 was a dog. Then the exhaust manifold got warped, and it sounded as mean as a dragster at the local dragstrip. Then came a couple of Ford E150 vans, both set up as campers with a bed, sink, and some storage. I lived in the mountains above Taos then, and only one car passed me on those roads, a 280 Z.

DAY FIFTEEN

A '78 Volvo 242 arrived, slow and unreliable, but safe.

My fastest, an '87 Chrysler LeBaron GTS with a turbo, before they became common. It cornered like it was on rails . . . when I could keep it out of the shop. Two Mustang ragtops brought a lot of fun. Knowing their strengths and weaknesses allowed me to trust them.

I drove each differently, to match its traits. That concept of trusting a vehicle went to new heights when I bought seven laps in a Lamborghini Gallardo 550 at Exotics Raceway, on a 1.8-mile road course with eight turns, one a tight hairpin. It was 550 horses, named after a Spanish bull.

I could trust hitting corners hard with no fear of tipping (a big concern with my vans) due to the low stance of the Gallardo, the grip of its tires, and low center of gravity. The course covered a section of the parking lot, so I had nothing to hit. But exiting a turn and hitting the gas too much too soon could cause a skid. Once I did that, and the back end broke loose some, but not too much. It was fun.

I could trust the braking. Megan, my instructor, taught me to avoid coasting by always either accelerating or braking. I could go in hot, a cone showed me where to brake, another cone where to straighten and hit the gas.

I could trust the manageable power of car to get me through the course quickly.

God's Way

In contrast to my no-go show boat Falcon, or my slow Volvo, I appreciated the power the Lambo provided. Earlier, I needed some extra spiritual power to change my deeply embedded selfishness. I had left God for some years of searching, and tried to change but could not.

Finally turning to God, I gave him full permission to do his stuff. Within a week, without me telling anyone, others asked what had changed in me. The secret to life-changing power? Our receiving and yielding to the Spirit. Jesus told his followers that we will receive power when the Holy Spirit comes to us (Acts 1:8). Let's explore living in the Spirit.

To access the Lambo's horses, I had to get in the car and turn on the key. Similarly, we need to get into Jesus. If you haven't yet, just ask him now to become your Savior and Lord. Next, the Lambo's power came by getting on the track and hitting the gas; we access the Spirit's power by getting into the Spirit's life: "Since we live by the Spirit, let us *keep in step with the Spirit*" (Galatians 5:25).

Step by step, moment by moment, we choose to build an awareness of his presence with us. We grasp that he's with us; we just have to remember that. But that can honestly sound a bit vague, so let's dig deeper into walking with the Spirit. Some call that being filled with the Spirit, and the apostle Paul described that: "*Be filled with the Spirit*, *speaking* to one another with psalms, hymns, and songs from the Spirit. Sing and make music from your heart to the Lord, always *giving thanks* to God the Father for everything, in the name of our Lord Jesus Christ. *Submit* to one another out of reverence for Christ." (Ephesians 5:18–21).

"Be filled" is the command, then he gave five participles, or steps, to being filled. The more we choose to do these, the more filled we get with the Spirit. Or the more the Spirit gets into us.

We *talk* about God stuff with our fellow believers and with others. I often end telemarketer phone calls with "God bless," and that always prompts a God awareness and, sometimes, nice conversations. We *sing* songs to and about God. Yesterday while fertilizing and weeding our lawn, I put some worship music on. We *give thanks*, because gratitude tightens our connection with him. Like before a meal. And we *put others' interests* on the same level as our own, the antidote to selfishness, and God moves more in our lives.

And as we do this, the Spirit brings more power into our lives. Trusted spiritual Lambo power.

DAY FIFTEEN

Crossing the Finish Line

How often do you sense the power of the Spirit in your life? With each temptation successfully resisted? With each song of praise you sing? Each time you serve someone? How can you grow in power?

DAY SIXTEEN

RUBY AND THE FUZZY COWS: MY HONDA VALKYRIE VISITS THE FUZZY COWS

Dan DeWitt

Dan DeWitt loves to experience new adventures. After serving as a pastor for many years, he is now enjoying the adventure of being retired and riding his motorcycle in the Ozark hills of southern Missouri.

After a long and cold Illinois winter, Ruby, my 2000 Honda Valkyrie, grew tired of the cold and was ready to fly. She longed for adventure, so I asked if she wanted to fly through the granite peaks, rolling grasslands, and clear mountain waters of Custer State Park in South Dakota. She didn't even spend a moment thinking about it before she said yes, so we began making plans.

Ruby thrilled when the corn fields of Illinois hit her rearview mirror. She was one bad dragon and felt the South Dakota Badlands must have been named just for her. Nothing could dim her spirits or hold her back as she flew through the Badlands. She was free, and she was happy.

We headed for Mount Rushmore and soon joined the throngs of tourists as they paid homage to the leaders of the past. She felt humbled as she considered the skill and effort required to carve those faces out of the granite mountains. It amazed her.

A short ride found us enjoying the switchbacks, pigtail bridges, and stone tunnels of Needles Highway and the Iron Mountain Road. Ruby hummed with delight with each passing moment. Our hearts beat as one, cruising down the roads and enjoying the beautiful vistas. Not even the thought of returning to the corn fields could dampen our spirits. Nothing could stop us now. We were free!

Little did we know that Custer State Park had a surprise in store. Our freewheeling ecstasy came to a dramatic end as Ruby the Dragon was to meet her match with a herd of fuzzy cows. At least that's what Ruby called the giant bison that roam the Custer State Park. Never in her life had she encountered man or beast who could challenge her prowess.

But at the center of the herd of fuzzy cows, right in the middle of the road, stood a massive bison bull denying passage to all. No matter how much Ruby huffed and puffed, the huge fuzzy cow was not deterred. Standing 6 feet tall and 12 feet long and weighing in at 2,000 pounds, this fuzzy cow showed no fear of Ruby—twice her size. And when he growled at her from up close, all of her bravado failed her. She had met her match and quickly yielded the road to the huge fuzzy cow. I must admit I had to shoot up a quick prayer to God.

In spite of that fuzzy cow obstacle that stood in our way, Ruby and I had a great trip. Now that we are back in the corn fields, I think I hear her rumble ever so slightly from time to time after I tuck her into bed at night. It makes me wonder if she is dreaming of her experience with the fuzzy cows, or maybe she is simply reliving the beauty of the trip. Either way, it was a grand adventure and we would do it again in a heartbeat!

Anyone with any sense would certainly get intimidated by a huge bison bull staring you down and bellowing at you. Even a mighty Honda Valkyrie! I can empathize. On a 2011 ride to the Lamar Valley in Yellowstone, a herd of bison crossed the road, then strolled in our direction. A bull on our right, a cow on our left, each within four feet or less. Yes, I've experienced intimidation by a bison too.

I suspect we've all faced intimidating situations in our lives. Family and friends and neighbors and coworkers who frighten, or attempt to frighten, us. Job situations that seem far beyond our ability to handle them successfully. War and combat. Going into a corner too hot and fear laying it down. All of these can easily intimidate us, or make us "timid or fearful, frighten, compel or deter by or as if by threats," according to Merriam Webster.

What intimidates us? Why? We'll focus on bringing God into our intimidating situations, regardless of their source. Apart from our personalities and resources. Kind of a generic, one-size-fits-all solution to intimidation.

Let's look into Joshua, the leader who followed Moses. Moses led them out of Egypt: Joshua was to lead them into the Promised Land, which we know as Israel. Joshua faced intimidation to an extent most of us cannot imagine.

First, following an established and revered leader brings tremendous comparison: "no prophet has risen in Israel like Moses, whom the Lord knew face to face" (Deuteronomy 34:10). Second, he had no trained soldiers; the Israelites had been slaves for centuries and had little experience with freedom and responsibility and courage. Third, the people were troublesome; two major leaders had led a rebellion against Moses, and the entire people followed it. Fourth, when they sent a reconnaissance party out, 10 of the 12 said they have no chance against the enemy.

That's intimidating; Joshua experienced it. The proof: Three times in verses 6, 7, and 9, God had to command Joshua to face intimidation with strength and courage. And with each, God taught how to do it.

"Be strong and courageous, because *you will lead these people to inherit the land*" (Joshua 1:6). Relying on God's promises kills intimidation when we trust them.

"Be strong and very courageous. *Be careful to obey all the law* my servant Moses gave you" (1:7). The more we align our lives with God, the more power we have to stand against intimidation.

"Be strong and courageous . . . for the LORD your God *will be with you* wherever you go" (1:9). With God at our back, in our lives, we can face anything.

To paraphrase a plaque in our house, "Sometimes the Lord calms the intimidator; sometimes he lets the intimidator rage and calms his child."

So when you face your bison bulls, follow God's three solutions.

Kick-Starting the Application

Think of a time when you felt intimidated. Did you bring God into it? Which of the three solutions works best for you? How can you face intimidation better?

DAY SEVENTEEN

TRUST YOURSELF

Speed's Way

Once we checked in at Exotics Racing, they shuffled us over to a classroom for some tips on driving our beasts. I checked out the competition—who would be fastest? All were younger, by far. Four months before 70, I knew my reactions had slowed down some, but as much as anything, I didn't want to embarrass myself. I'd test-driven some nice sports cars but always on city streets. A race-bred Lotus Elan topped the list, but I'd driven Porsches, a Vette, a Z, and a few others. None all out, never pushing them fully in the turns.

This would be my first ride in a true supercar. First ride on a course. Not an oval, but a 1.8-mile track with eight turns, somewhat like my hometown Long Beach Grand Prix. I had dreamed of driving a Lambo for decades but still felt intimidated. I'd never used a paddle shifter, never had a trained instructor sitting by my side telling me what to do or not do . . . except driver training in high school.

Gotta give Exotics credit, they gave detailed instructions: Two cars would be on the track at the same time and our onboard instructor would let us know if a car wanted to pass us so we could slow down and pull over; we also covered cornering, the paddle shifter, the role of the instructor, and all. Then the intimidation increased. The instructors hopped in their car of the day, warmed them up, then hit the track, all at once. They said they did it to warm up the tires and engines fully, but they impressed us with their skill. The roar of 12 high-performance engines vibrated our hearts. Could we do that? No way. My takeaway? Intimidation.

Another Lambo had entered the course a lap before me, a newer model with more horsepower. They encouraged us to go slow the first lap or two to get the feel of the car and course. I pulled onto the track, where the concentration required surprised me, and Megan kept giving tips. Then the other Lambo approached our rear, as Megan tapped me on the shoulder. Dang, that embarrassed this competitive lover of speed! I slowed, he passed and pulled well ahead, then Megan whispered, "Go for it." My speed increased. I started to feel comfortable, then a lap later saw the other Lambo just ahead.

To my delight, he slowed and pulled over as I blew past him. I never saw him again. If I'd seen him after, I would have greeted him with a proud smile on my face.

Afterward, we viewed some videos that showed our speed, and I reached 112 on the straight that ended in a hairpin, 170-degree turn. Yes. I could do this. I learned to trust myself in a supercar on a tough course, and I came out on top.

God's Way

So what does it take to trust ourselves on the spiritual track? We've read the passages, "*The heart is deceitful* above all things and beyond cure" (Jeremiah 17:9), or "If we *claim to be without sin*, we deceive ourselves and the truth is not in us" (1 John 1:8). They don't really build much confidence in ourselves, so maybe we need to rethink this concept.

I love the line that insanity means doing the same thing while expecting a different result. Well, our brokenness and flaws and sin nature got us into the spiritual mess we are all in, so let's look at Paul's source of spiritual trust:

> We "*put no confidence in the flesh*—though I myself have reasons for such confidence. If someone else thinks they have reasons to put confidence in the flesh, I have more:

> circumcised on the eighth day, of the people of Israel, of the tribe of Benjamin, a Hebrew of Hebrews; in regard to the law, a Pharisee; as for zeal, persecuting the church; as for righteousness based on the law, faultless. But whatever were gains to me I now consider loss for the sake of Christ" (Philippians 3:3–7).

Paul did all he possibly could but concluded he'd wasted his time trusting in what he could do. Paul's conclusion: We can't trust ourselves to do enough good, to be good enough.

We all eventually come to that conclusion. For me, my innate selfishness proved stronger than I, which began my journey with God. This realization can come before we decide to follow, or even at some point along the track of life. Many times, I thought I could handle things on my own, only to fail. Stupendously. Actually, that's good. We learn we can't trust ourselves, that we can't put any confidence in what we do ourselves to be righteous.

God smiles when we grasp that; he's been waiting in the pits with a turbocharger to install. The passage above continues to describes that:

> "I consider everything a loss because of the surpassing worth of knowing Christ Jesus my Lord, for whose sake I have lost all things. I consider them garbage, that I may gain Christ and be found in him, *not having a righteousness of my own* that comes from the law, but that which is through faith in Christ—*the righteousness that comes from God* on the basis of faith. I want to know Christ—yes, to know the power of his resurrection and participation in his sufferings, becoming like him in his death, and so, somehow, attaining to the resurrection from the dead" (Philippians 3:8–11).

We get Christ in our lives, get covered in the fire suit of God's righteousness, and possess the same Holy Spirit power that raised Jesus from death. With the Spirit guiding and teaching us, we have the power to resist temptation. We grow into Christlikeness step by step. We have the wisdom to make good choices in life.

And we can trust ourselves to arrive at the finish line. Not by our innate power but by Jesus living in us.

Crossing the Finish Line

When did you first realize you didn't have the ability to trust in yourself spiritually? Have you dealt with that by daily giving God permission to lead and change you? What keeps you from that?

DAY EIGHTEEN

SLIP AWAY: FINDING SERENITY ON THE ROAD

Bikers have a saying, "You rarely see motorcycles parked outside a psychiatrist's office." I love that! This series' second book, *More God, Motorcycles, and Open Roads*, published in 2024, shared some studies that showed what we call "wind therapy" works. The act of riding itself decreases stress, and we all crave relief from the responsibilities and demands and issues and pressures of life. But in this book, let's follow a slightly different method. A little more reason about why it works.

The bike well packed
and ready to ride to
    the Montana mountains
        still snowcapped
    the varied North Dakota hills
    the North Woods of Minnesota
        with abandoned homes
        on functioning farms
with birch hinting that fall comes soon
I slip away from
    to-do lists
    bills to pay
    worries and responsibilities

concerns
all have their day
but not this one
and the absence of the former
and the presence of the latter
brings serenity to my soul
So I slip away

Life in America can get hectic. Many husbands and wives both work, many have two jobs to pay the bills. Inflation has slowed down from its heights, but the prices haven't returned to their earlier levels. Political division in America continues to stress many.

Our lives get crammed full of obligations, necessary ones. Bills to pay. Tasks to complete. Relationships to maintain. Helping others. Serving God in and outside church. When they consume our time and energy and resources, our soul seems to shrink. Little time to ponder and meditate and grow, to see the deeper realities of life: God, ourselves, our place in life.

An article "Stress in America" (Seth J. Gillihan, PhD, *Psychology Today*, June 7, 2022) explored how stress has reached "alarming levels" and increasingly afflicts our culture and our people. Defined as mental, physical, or emotional demands on our resources, stress shows itself in social withdrawal, exhaustion, depression, burnout, physical illness, muscle tension, poor sleep, headaches, and digestive problems. Any of those sound familiar?

May we never forget the precious promise of Jesus, "In this world you *will have trouble*" (John 16:33). By its nature, life stresses us in a multitude of ways. It just seems to get worse.

Jesus faced that dilemma as he began his ministry. In starting this Day, I had some ideas of where to go. But only on the third draft did this next aspect come in. Jesus likely had a pretty good idea of how vigorous and rigorous and difficult his ministry would be. He'd be a temporary rock star, everyone wanted something from him. He also knew the next step. He, who had been wholly holy, would go beyond taking on our sin and become sin, "God made him who had no sin to *be sin* for us" (2 Corinthians 5:21).

Jesus became sin. I can't grasp that, but he knew that was coming. So how did he prepare for all the stress of his ministry and sacrifice?

His first public exposure came with his baptism by his cousin John the Baptizer, then the Father had his Spirit step in: "Then Jesus was led by the Spirit into the wilderness to be tempted by the devil. After fasting forty days and forty nights, he was hungry" (Matthew 4:1–2). Notice the order: Led by the Spirit, Jesus slipped away, then spent 40 days fasting to strengthen his connection with his Father. Only then did the final purpose arrive: temptation. We often talk about the temptations, maybe touch on a long time without food, but we skip over the intimacy increased with God in the 40 days *before* the temptations.

So Jesus slipped away to get close to God, to endure the worst temptations, in order to handle the stresses of his about-to-begin ministry.

Jesus faced that same dilemma of stress during his ministry, being drained by demands from the people he came to touch. His response? To slip away: "But Jesus *often withdrew* to lonely places and prayed" (Luke 5:16; see also 6:12, 9:18, 9:28, 11:1). Frequently, those escapes followed heavy ministry times, like after the feeding of the 5,000. A time to restore after being drained emotionally and physically. So he got away and prayed.

Why should we slip away, in whatever manner works for us?

First, we give our body a chance to rest. God ordained, and exemplified, a day of rest. We need that.

Second, we can focus better on God with fewer distractions. We can pick up his whispers.

Third, we give ourselves chances to meditate and ponder, to strategize on the long term.

Long bike trips work for me. I turn off the music, maybe sing, certainly pray, and meditate on how to do it all better. Journeys to the mountains and the beach do the same. Sheila and I often get refreshed taking two chairs to a local beach for a day, to just sit and soak. Maybe read. Maybe nap. Maybe converse. Maybe take a stroll. Many days I write in the morning, do yard work in the early afternoon, then grab a book and a beer and sit by our backyard waterfall. I slip away from the stressors. Even short slips away can restore us.

We each need to find how we slip away, either for weeks or days or hours. But we must find our way to slip away, however we do it. I suggest intentionally strategizing before the demands fill up your schedule, before the stress builds too high. Schedule in some times. Spontaneously slip away when the stress gets high or when you have the chance.

If it worked for Jesus, it might just work for us.

Kick-Starting the Application

Do the obligations of life often weigh you down? What have you found works best for you to slip away? Do you regularly carve out time for it? What might God be hinting at for you?

DAY NINETEEN

TASTE AND SEE

Karl Smith

Karl is an architect, a transportation designer and researcher, and a journalist living in Thousand Oaks, California. Fascinated by both the past and the future of the car, he has written extensively about both. He and his wife Leilani share a love of art, music, and travel.

Speed's Way

A cold, overcast day in an Alabama winter hardly seems like an occasion for a life-changing epiphany, but it happened to me when my friend Matt cornered me outside my high school history class and said, "C'mon, I've got something to show you."

Curious, I followed him out to the student parking lot to see a silver and black Porsche 914 sitting incongruously among the old beaters and mom-wagons my classmates drove.

Enchanted, I helped Matt remove the Targa top. I eased myself into the passenger seat and buckled up. As Matt fired up the motor, I felt the strong vibration of the engine behind us. Easing out of the parking lot so as to not draw too much attention to ourselves, we cruised through the neighborhoods and then streaked out onto the highway.

DAY NINETEEN

Despite the chilly weather, the ride was incredible. The boxer engine, sounding like something between a purr and a growl, wasn't even straining at high speeds. Our eyes were level with the lug nuts on the large trucks as we flashed by. The guardrails were a blur, and our backsides soon became all too familiar with the texture of the pavement and every bump in the road.

As we wound through the hills, the tires screeched as Matt slammed through the curves. All around us, the road was lined with rocky outcroppings, little waterfalls of winter rainwater, a leafless forest—it was magical. The passing landscape seemed so much larger, more immediate, more visceral. Compared to riding in my parents' cushy family cars, the Porsche was an introduction to a much larger world, even though it came in a very small but nimble package.

When we returned the car, the owner, Jeff, greeted us. After introductions, Jeff asked me, "Did you drive my little German rocket?"

"No, I answered, sheepishly. "I can't afford a car right now."

I didn't want him to know that I didn't even have my license yet.

"Well, drive it around the property anyway; at least you will get a taste of sports car ownership."

I crept along in first gear around the roads that led to his barn, sheds, and pasture. On my return Jeff said, "Well, that wasn't much, but at least you got a taste."

Grinning ear to ear, I said, "Yes, sir! Wonderful!"

As Matt and I drove away, I thought of one of the scriptures we had been studying in a youth group at church, Psalm 34:8: "Taste and see that the LORD is good; blessed is the one who takes refuge in him."

Though I couldn't know it then, that taste of sports car ownership would lead to a banquet of love for all things automotive and would ultimately change the course of my career.

And that verse from the psalms? It has stayed close to me over the years too. A taste of the Lord's goodness and mercy has led to a lifetime banquet of love and blessings from our Father, and I am profoundly grateful.

DAY NINETEEN

God's Way

I absolutely love Karl's writing and insights; truly, we need to taste God, to experience him. But for many, something must come first. For Karl, a friend invited him. For others, before tasting God, we need some assurance that God truly exists and that Jesus's claim to be the only path to God has substance. The resurrection of Jesus provides that. No resurrection, no Christianity: "And if Christ has not been raised, our preaching is useless and so is your faith . . . And if Christ has not been raised, your faith is futile; you are still in your sins" (1 Corinthians 15:14, 17). Please read the entire passage, verses 12 to 19. The Sunday before I wrote this, our pastor talked about the proofs of the resurrection of Jesus three days after his death (Chris Brown, North Coast Church, Vista, CA). Let's look at some briefly, then we'll start the taste test.

1. We have four eyewitness biographies from the time and place (Matthew, Mark, Luke, and John).
2. Numerous nonbiblical sources state the empty tomb claim. Josephus, a Jewish general who went over to the Romans, said in 97 AD, "He appeared to them alive again the third day" (*Antiquities of the Jews*, chap. III, para. 3).
3. Critics had to claim the body was stolen, because the reality of the empty grave was common knowledge. They had to find some explanation.
4. After the crucifixion the apostles hid in fear, but after the resurrection they became a spiritual force that turned the world upside down (Acts 17:6 NKJV). Only John escaped martyrdom; he merely faced exile.
5. Paul's life was changed from killing Christians to become the top church planter in the world, and he became a martyr because of his faith. The change agent? He saw the resurrected Jesus (Acts 22:1–21).

But believing the right things about Jesus, that he is the Son of God, and even doing good things for him won't get us to Jesus, the Father, or heaven, according to Jesus: "Many will say to me on that day, 'Lord, Lord, did we not prophesy in your name and in your name drive out demons and in your name perform many miracles?' Then I will tell them plainly, 'I never knew you. Away from me, you evildoers!" (Matthew 7:22–24).

A harsh claim, and Jesus's brother goes even further: "You believe that there is one God. Good! Even the demons believe that—and shudder" (James 2:19). Jesus desires more than intellectual belief but that we taste him, like Wayne did in his story above. A taste that led to a new life. An experience, not just information. A taste that leads to an eternal banquet.

Jesus wants followers, friends, people who know him personally, as Savior and Lord: "Now this is *eternal life*: that they *know you*, the only true God, and Jesus Christ, whom you have sent" (John 17:3). If you yet haven't done this, I prayerfully encourage you to do so.

Crossing the Finish Line

Do you know about Jesus, maybe even serve him, but not know him personally? What keeps you from that? Are you willing to taste and see that the Lord is good? Then get to know him as Lord and resurrected Savior.

DAY TWENTY

DON'T TRUST YOUR EXPERIENCES

Speed's Way

For some of the six years we lived in Newbury Park, while teaching English at Oaks Christian High School I also taught night classes at Oxnard College, about 17 miles west on Potrero Road, the old Conejo Grade. Two miles were steep and winding, with six good curves and several more sweeping ones—an ideal road for my Mustang ragtop. Going downhill at about 6:00 p.m. traffic would clog the road, so I patiently cruised in line.

Returning uphill at 10:0 p.m. brought a different experience: no traffic at all. I could let the Mustang be the sports car Ford designed. When approaching a curve, I let off the gas to decrease my speed. That saved braking lining, but I'd learned that braking while turning doesn't give you optimal control.

Sports car mags then said the shortest distance came when hugging the inner part of the curve, so I kept my tires close to the inside. I'd maintain that through the turn with a little gas, then accelerate after the apex out of the curve and set up for the next delightful twisty.

No one ever caught or passed me on that road, and I felt pretty confident about my cornering abilities. Then came the ride on a Lamborghini Gallardo 550 at Exotics Racing.

I knew the Lambo had far more horses than I'd ever driven but thought that just gave faster acceleration! Until we pulled out on the course, and I used my experience and eased off on the gas at the first curve. "No!" came Megan's instant response. "Never coast. Your foot belongs on either the gas or brake pedals; no coasting." My old experiences had taken over. This Lambo and course were different; this wasn't just going fast but a race. You don't want to lose a fraction of a second. Coasting kills your time.

That made sense, but it took multiple laps for me to move instantly from gas to brake to gas. That also increased the amount of concentration required.

The next issue arrived when, like always, I turned into the turn, wanting to hug the entire inner curve. Another "No!" That was the shortest distance in a turn but the slowest. The class had diagrammed the best turn: Stay straight as long as possible, and don't initiate braking or turning too soon. Accelerate until the first orange cone, brake, then turn in one move to the apex of the turn (a cone was there to help), and at the third cone turn straight into the center of the lane and accelerate . . . but not too much or the 550 horses would put you in a skid.

Instead on one long sweeping turn, you make two quick ones and maintain more speed. Why? The Lambo turns and accelerates and holds its grip better than any of my cars had ever done. The Lambo could do it; my Mustang could not.

Frankly, my experiences with other cars became useless in the Lambo on a road course. And more than useless, they hurt my driving.

God's Way

That same process hampered my spiritual life. Oh, it helped me accept Jesus as Lord and Savior. It helped me make better decisions in life. It helped provide good friends at church in the youth groups earlier and the adult groups later. But spiritually, I drove through life in an okay Honda Accord, not a Lamborghini Gallardo 550.

DAY TWENTY

Three misconceptions hindered me, maybe you can identify. I suspect many will.

First, I focused too much on my behavior. In part, that was typical growing up in church in the 1950s and '60s. That causes several problems: We tend to hide or ignore or deny our issues, which we avoid by grasping that our behavioral acts don't bring us to God: "For it is by grace you have been saved, *through faith*—and this is not from yourselves, it is the gift of God—*not by works*, so that no one can boast. For we are God's handiwork, created in Christ Jesus to do good works" (Ephesians 2:8–10).

Yes, behavior counts; God created us to do good, but good follows faith. The key solution came when I grasped that faith means relationship: "Now this is eternal life: that they *know you*, the only true God, and Jesus Christ" (John 17:3). That intimacy with the Creator defines our faith, not primarily our behavior.

Second, and linked to that, I took too much responsibility for spiritual strength. The changes that God made gave me a confidence that didn't match reality. Not long after this, I let myself get into two situations that I thought I could handle, but the temptations blasted me. Those failings showed the solution, to rely on the power of the Spirit who now lived in me: "But you will *receive power* when the Holy Spirit comes on you; and you will be my witnesses in Jerusalem, and in all Judea and Samaria, and to the ends of the earth" (Acts 1:8).

The more areas I let Jesus into as Lord let him possess more of me.

Third, I became overly judgmental, stressing truth over grace, not fully understanding that "the law was given through Moses, but *grace and truth* came through Jesus Christ" (John 1:17 NKJV). Truth carries importance; Jesus described himself as "the truth" in John 14:6. Genuine faith must be based on what the Spirit caused to be written in scripture.

But by holding onto truth too strongly, I minimized grace in relationships. That hurt my connections with fellow believers—looking down on them—because I did not "make every effort to keep the unity of the Spirit through the bond of peace" (Ephesians 4:3). Grace with truth has the power to connect us more strongly to one another, once more providing spiritual power.

I had to discard some of my previous experiences in order to live the Lambo life in Christ.

Crossing the Finish Line

Do you have some earlier experiences that hinder your walk with Jesus? What are they? How can you reformulate them into more effective traits? Will you?

DAY TWENTY-ONE

WHEN A PANCAKE BREAKFAST GOES SOUTH: BEING GRACIOUS WHEN SINNERS ACT LIKE SINNERS

Libby Taylor-Worden

Libby Taylor-Worden is a fiction author of two books, Port of Refuge *and* Listening. *Her first book is a story of motorcycle ministry within the 1 percent motorcycle culture.*

The first Saturday of each month a local motorcycle club hosts a pancake breakfast. Rain or shine my husband and I attended. Once we arrived early and I was told, "That's *very special* coffee." I quickly learned their first pot of coffee included a pick-me-up for the club members who partied late the night before.

One month my sister Cyndi was visiting. I gave her the option to sleep late or join us for the pancake breakfast. My husband rode and we followed in a car into the foothills. It had rained the night before, but tables and chairs were set up on the damp cement deck in back of the clubhouse. Bikes filled the parking lot. Several clubs and two motorcycle ministry patches were present. It was good to see friends after a rough winter with lots of events canceled. I greeted many friends and introduced my sister around.

Once seated with our breakfast of pancakes, eggs, and sausage, Cyndi engaged openly in conversation with others. Somehow the topic of drugs came up, and Cyndi's voice went up an octave to declare her opinion of drugs, the people who do drugs, and those who sell drugs.

"Cyndi, quiet."

"Why? It's true," she broadcasted as if she'd recited a rehearsed position she had often repeated whenever the topic was raised.

"Stop talking. Now! Or we're leaving," I pleaded.

She opened her mouth for a rebuttal, but I headed her off, whispering, "Stop! Now!" I pulled back my chair as if about to stand to reinforce my ultimatum.

She returned a whispered, "Okay, okay." Puzzled but obedient, she fell silent and others changed the subject. In the car on the way home I explained my actions to quell her curiosity. She sat silently listening to ministry basics I had neglected to mention on the drive up.

"Remember before I knew Jesus and Joyce declared, 'You're a sinner and unless you repent, you're going to hell'?" Cyndi nodded. "Do you remember how that affected me?"

"You and Joyce didn't speak for two years."

"Many club members not only do drugs; some also sell drugs. But God doesn't call us to judge them. God calls us to love them and show them—through our actions—that God loves them." I went on to explain that we don't attend events to check off our to-do list: Ate with sinners. We don't set out to convict them of their sins. It's not our job to do the work of the Holy Spirit. Our job is to love them in spite of their lifestyle.

Then I shared Ephesians 4:32 (NASB 1995): "Be kind to one another, tender-hearted, forgiving each other, just as God in Christ also has forgiven you." I reminded her that I am a sinner who spent two years in rebellion to hellfire and brimstone but later came to know Jesus once I was introduced to the gospel of love and acceptance.

DAY TWENTY-ONE

Libby brought up a difficult issue: How do we deal with people who sin grossly? Her sister took a stand on drugs. Loudly, vociferously, judgmentally. Many who follow Jesus do the same, but this brings three major problems.

First, it creates a false division between people. We who follow Jesus can assume we have an intrinsically different human nature than those who do not. When we look down on those who sin apart from Jesus, we ignore that we all sin. John, the favored apostle, put us all in one group: "If we say that we have no sin, we deceive ourselves, and the truth is not in us" (1 John 1:8 ESV). We and those in gross sin may differ in how we sin, but we belong to the same family. Frankly, that brings some needed humility.

Just one sin puts us in the group of sinners. Just one sin puts us in the category of needing Jesus to take care of our sin.

Second, we create a false distinction when we put sinners on a continuum of who's worse. We condemn drug dealers and child abusers. Yes, some sins have a greater impact than others. But right after the most famous verse in the Bible, Jesus defined the ultimate sin, the one that determines our eternal destiny: "For God so loved the world that he gave his one and only Son, that whoever believes in him shall not perish but have eternal life . . . Whoever believes in him is not condemned, but whoever does not believe stands condemned already because they have not believed in the name of God's one and only Son." (John 3:16, 18).

Believing in Jesus as Savior and Lord determines destiny. If we do, we go up. If we don't, we go down. So why do we focus on some sins and judge and reject people when we need to focus on knowing Jesus? Why do we try to change people's behavior apart from coming to Jesus? If they act better, hell merely gets nicer people. That's the only difference.

Let's focus less on changing their behavior and more on changing their relationship with Jesus. The latter has the most importance. The former will come later. We'll never reach sinless, but we can sin less.

Legalism and judgmentalism lead to the third error: false communication. When we focus on behavior, we get harsh. When we focus on following, we exude the same grace we received: "And the Lord's servant must not be quarrelsome but must be kind to everyone, able to teach, not resentful. Opponents must be gently instructed, in the hope that God will grant them repentance leading them to a knowledge of the truth, and that they will come to their senses and escape from the trap of the devil, who has taken them captive to do his will" (2 Timothy 2:24–26).

Hellfire and brimstone drove Libby away. Love and acceptance brought her to Jesus. May we spread that.

Kick-Starting the Application

What sins by others make you resistant to show love and acceptance to them as a person? Do you tend to be argumentative in discussions, or gracious? How can you be a better conduit for God's grace to sinners?

DAY TWENTY-TWO

BLOWN AWAY BY MY MIATA

Leilani Strong Smith

Leilani Smith is a Jesus-loving science teacher. When not teaching, she is writing her devotional for those living with chronic illness. She looks for joy, beauty, and grace in the hardship of living with Adult-onset Still's disease (AOSD.

Speed's Way

My friend invited me to her home north along the coast in order to see my newly purchased red 1990 Miata. The thought of driving the two and a half hours to her city sounded thrilling! Before I embarked from Thousand Oaks, California, I lowered the Miata's top, donned my Italian sunglasses, and cued up the loud Cuban music. I took one more look in the rearview mirror to make sure my pink-dyed hair and fire-engine red lipstick were in proper order. My eagerness to feel the wind in my hair, to see the country views of vineyards and horses, to experience the curves of the road to Santa Maria, and to enjoy the shifting of the manual drive gave a visceral experience of which I never tired.

About an hour into the trip I reached Carpinteria; the traffic thinned and the magic started. The scent of the ocean saltwater, the flock of pelicans flying parallel to me, and the sound of the conga drums captivated my soul. "Thank you, Lord, for your blessings," I whispered.

DAY TWENTY-TWO

A few miles before I was to exit the main highway to take the country bypass, I stopped at a fast-food restaurant to use the facilities because there were no modern conveniences on the isolated backroad.

Thankfully, the bathroom was empty, and I did not have to wait for a stall. I exited it thinking I would arrive before dinner. Lost in my thoughts of wondering what my friend would be serving, I stared in shock at my reflection in the mirror as I washed my hands: My pink hair was gone! "What?!" Then I started laughing. You see, pink is not absorbed into the hair shaft as other colors are. Instead, it sits on the surface of the hair. My beautiful pink hair was blown away by the joy ride in my Miata.

As I wended my way through the rural terrain, the sun's golden hour started. Horses headed toward their barns. A tractor slowed the single lane going north. In the hills to the northeast, the bright California poppies blew me kisses and wished me Godspeed. I relaxed knowing that my friend's house was 30 minutes away. The pleasure of driving alone . . . in a Miata. You should try it sometime.

I pulled into my friend's driveway, and she met me at the door. "Where's your pink hair?" she queried. "I lost it somewhere on the road! I'll explain later. Come see my little red rocket."

After dinner, she asked if we could drive mid-morning from the beach to the Rancho Sisquoc Winery. "We can pack a picnic lunch. There are a lot of tight curves and dips in the road to get to the winery. It's out in the middle of nowhere. Do you mind if we take the Miata with the top down?"

I told her, "Of course, but be prepared to be blown away!"

God's Way

Leilani presented me with a great story, using '60s terminology: God will blow us away with the changes and opportunities that he brings. That fits well, since we're focusing on adventures on our spiritual travels, with one of my wife's favorite verses: "What no eye has seen, what no ear has heard, and what no human mind has conceived—the things God has prepared for those who love him" (1 Corinthians 2:9).

Or we can't begin to imagine the good stuff that God has personally designed for us. I titled my first novel *Wild Rides*, because my paternal family had some wild rides, both good and bad. But when we love Jesus, God provides a wild and good ride beyond our dreams.

First, he makes us a new person. My failings, and inability to fix them, motivated me to try Jesus. I remember praying at 23, "God, I give you permission to change anything you want. If this works, I'm with you forever; if not, I'm gone." Within a week, without me telling anyone about this, people began asking what had happened. Before I knew the verse, I knew the reality that "anyone who belongs to Christ has *become a new person*. The old life is gone; a new life has begun!" (2 Corinthian 5:17 NLT)

Theologians describe the soul, or our individual person, as our mind, emotions, and will. It blows me away that my thought life has changed so much, away from a focus on my own needs and desires, with more care for others. My emotions have become more stable and positive, less driven by impulse. And my decision-making has new values, based on scripture and God's heart, to guide me on what path to choose.

Yes, I'm the same person, Tim Riter, but Tim Riter as a new creation, a new person. We all experience this.

He also blows us away with giving us a purpose that transcends benefitting ourselves. We get a reason for living that goes beyond our innate self-centeredness: "Do nothing out of selfish ambition or vain conceit. Rather, in humility value others above yourselves, not looking to your own interests but each of you to the interests of the others" (Philippians 2:3–4).

We transcend ourselves by acting like Jesus, caring about other's needs.

One more blow-away comes from how he guides us through life into situations we could never dream of. A classic passage explores this: "A man's mind plans his way, but the LORD directs his steps" (Proverbs 16:9 RSV). Until 30, I worked but with little purpose except to pay the bills. Then God led me into the ministry, which prepared me for writing. Earlier, I dreamed of getting one book published, now 14 have been done. Just one example of God exceeding our dreams.

So please enjoy your ride with Jesus. He will blow you away!

Crossing the Finish Line

Have you experienced God blowing you away with changes in your person, purpose, and practices? Have you given him full permission to change you? If not, now is the time to cross the line.

DAY TWENTY-THREE

OLD DOGS AND NEW TRICKS

In my early years, in all aspects of life, I relied on youth and vigor and a strong body. At 26 came a 31-state, 13,000-mile ride on a naked semi-chopped Honda CB750. Naked doesn't refer to my riding apparel; it means no fairing, no windshield, no attached bags, no power ports, no radio, no sound, no cruise control, no Cramp Buster. Just a basic bike. A duffle bag served as a backrest. Semi-chopped with a 6-inch extension on the front forks. It did have highway pegs.

The longest single-day ride stretched between Beaumont and El Paso, all in Texas, well over 800 miles. Stops only for gas and meals. A lot of nothing . . . just me and circling vultures. And I loved it! *Then.* But I've picked up some new tricks along the way, some by necessity.

My current ride, a 2014 Honda CTX, came with a lot of features: fairing and windshield, ABS brakes, saddlebags. But before May's 2024 ride to Idaho with Jerry, covering just seven states and under 3,000 miles, I made some changes. This old dog learned some new tricks, since his body 50 years later didn't remain the same. Nor did technology.

An aftermarket windshield with an air wing at the top diverted more air for better protection. Highway pegs allowed me to stretch my legs. An aftermarket cruise control saved my wrist. A passenger backrest backstopped my duffle bag for a comfy backrest. A cup holder allowed frequent hydration, and an added cell phone charger outlet and a cell phone mount provided Waze directions. And while gas stops reached 250 miles before, they now max at 150 miles, preferably 120.

Why? My body at 76 just couldn't do what it did at 26. Twenty years back I tore the meniscus and ACL in my left knee, and it cries out for stretching more than the highway pegs afford; that means I have to get off the bike. My back complains about remaining in one position on the seat too long. Yeah, I have four sitting positions on the bike, and they help, but not enough. And while I did a 16-hour, 1,080-mile ride at 70, that meant extra tiredness stayed for days.

No longer the young dog, this old dog has decided to learn some new tricks. I can't ride like before but I want to still ride, so I ride differently to account for my changing body and changing technology. Fifty years ago, that 750 had the newest technology possible, but we have more options today, like cruise control on bikes. Like ABS. Like power outlets for Waze. Like fuel injection for better gas mileage. Like integrated fairings and windshields. Why should we live in the past when we have better options? I want to learn, to adapt. As I write this, my long-time friend and riding buddy Jerry is selling his Goldwing to get a smaller bike, easier to handle so he can still ride.

At some point, I may also have to downsize in order to keep riding. But not yet.

Wise people and institutions, like churches or businesses or groups learn to adapt to changing circumstances. A few months back, I had a fine discussion on Facebook with a good friend, Jeff Boyer, about how the bigger a group (nation, church, business, whatever) gets, the more organization they need to stay effective.

We also see that with the constantly changing technology. My first computer at our church had no hard drive: just two floppy disks. We inserted one for the program, then another containing files to use on that program. And we had to type in a long log-in URL every time we turned it on. We thought we had all the best stuff! Until a newer version came out, and a newer one, and on and on and on.

After Pentecost, the new Jerusalem church simply met in homes and listened to the apostles. That worked for then and for them. But the church began to spread out to new territories, and when Paul planted a church in a city, he was the leader. His goal was to plant new churches all over, so he would often appoint one of his coworkers to become the new pastor leader when he moved on, like he did with Timothy and the church in Ephesus and with Titus in Crete.

But as time went on, Paul encouraged Timothy and Titus to appoint elders and deacons in each town. Why? The churches grew beyond the ability of just one person to oversee them (see 1 Timothy 3 and Titus 1:5). Like Jeff mentioned, those fellowships required more structure, like elders and deacons. The church adapted.

That principle of adapting also applies to communication methods. When talking to Jewish folks, Paul quoted the Old Testament that they knew. When talking to Gentiles without that background, he quoted their philosophers and religious beliefs. He adapted the method to the audience.

Realize that old dogs can learn new tricks. Realize that changing situations often require new strategies to more effectively live as strangers in a strange land. Let's be progressive in that. But it comes with a caveat. If we merely adapt to the culture, we can lose the power of the message. We don't tell people what they want to hear, but we tell them, in a culturally relevant manner, what God wants them to hear.

We use God's unchanging word as our template for the message and use his principles on when and how to flex. As we do that, we can better affect the world for God. We can all learn some new tricks.

Kick-Starting the Application

How do you keep up with changes? Do you tend to accept them, or do you question them or reject them? How well do you use God's word as the standard to evaluate the changes? What's one change you need to consider right now to better honor God?

DAY TWENTY-FOUR

CHANGING OUR PAST?

Speed's Way

Driving home after my Lambo exhilaration in our reliable Honda Accord with my wife, I pondered some new concepts. First, this experience unexpectedly changed me. My views on what I could handle in a car grew, and a tease tickled my brain of doing more. As a part of that, my love of speed increased. The adrenaline rush of handling a supercar through the curves and straights made me desire more. The idea of pursuing this tempted me.

Second, I realized this could become a book. I'd done one motorcycle-based devotional that did well, opening at number one in Motorcycle New Releases on Amazon. I mentioned that to my wife, and she replied, "Can you get enough ideas for a book?"

A fair question, so I rattled off half a dozen or so on the spot. That got me more enthused, and this devo combining motorcycles and sports cars shows the fruit of the seed of that day in 2017. Yeah, a lot of thoughts grow into book ideas. This is book 14; two more are in the works and 20 or so proposals can be found in my files. I'm a book guy.

But another idea struck me. This experience exponentially increased my love of going fast, and I was decent at it. I passed a much younger driver in a faster car and hit 112 in a straight that led into a hairpin curve. While driving my full-sized Ford vans in the Taos mountains, only one car, a Z sports car, passed me. Dad held the Cannonball Run record, which left a mark on me. But no, at 69 I wasn't about to leave retirement and compete on a sports car circuit. That train had left the station.

But I did wonder: If I had tried this 50 years earlier, could I have made the switch? Don't we all do that? We look back and wonder, "What if I'd gone to college? What if Gayle had introduced me to Cheryl Ladd? What if I hadn't . . ." You get the picture. But we don't get do-overs. We can't go back. What's done is done. Life is as it is.

But we can learn by looking back. We figure out the values we had when we made various decisions. Have those values changed? Can we, should we, resurrect that option from earlier? In the midst of this, I picked up a core value that helps me navigate life—and might help you too.

God's Way

As we ponder past decisions, what we should have or should not have made, as we choose our life's direction, or purpose, or mission, God says we choose one of two options that will set the course of our lives, that will determine if God grades our lives as successful or not. Simply, do we choose to please God or to please ourselves?

Early on, I chose to please God, but frankly, it was half-hearted. A friend described me in those days as "though loving the Lord, living your life." Frankly, that is impossible if we truly want to please God. Even then, I chewed on a church in the book of Revelation, Laodicea, which didn't please Jesus: "I know your deeds, that you are *neither cold nor hot.* I wish you were either one or the other! So, *because you are lukewarm*—neither hot nor cold—I am *about to spit you out* of my mouth" (Revelation 3:15–16).

My spiritual temp was lukewarm, neither hot nor cold. The danger: We have enough warmth to think we're not cold but not enough to be hot. Jesus commands: "You shall love the LORD your God with *all your heart, with all your soul, and with all your mind*"

(Matthew 22:37). That's hot: the desire to put Jesus first as both our Savior and Lord.

Loving him like this means we obey, that we choose to follow his mission: "All authority in heaven and on earth has been given to me. Therefore go and *make disciples* of all nations, *baptizing* them in the name of the Father and of the Son and of the Holy Spirit, and *teaching* them to obey everything I have commanded you" (Matthew 28:18–20). My pastor, Chris Brown of North Coast Church in Vista, California, calls this choosing to build God's kingdom or our kingdom.

When I got this concept, I moved from "though loving the Lord, living your life" to "loving the Lord and living his life."

And this gives the link to the story of me trading places: my current life or having giving it to racing. Note: This is how this worked out in my life. The specifics will vary, but all followers should have this goal. That said, we really can't have this goal unless we deeply grasp how different pleasing God is from pleasing self.

Another life-changing passage in Romans 8:1–10 helped me see this. I encourage you to read it yourself, but here's a summary of the distinctions of living for self or for God:

Please Sinful Self	**Please God**
3 sin is condemned	1 no condemnation
4 live by sin nature, please self	2 free from law
5 mindset on sin	4 live by Spirit
6 brings death	5 mindset on Spirit gain life and peace
7 opposed to God	9 controlled by Spirit
8 cannot please God	10 Christ in you, spiritually alive
9 controlled by sin nature, cannot please God	

Back in my 20s, I realized this huge gap. For me, just me, getting into racing would have been to please me. I would have loved it. And while I could not have blended the two, many can. We can build God's kingdom in almost any profession when our heart desires to please God, to build his kingdom with our gifts and resources. Yes, have fun. Enjoy life. But build your life on pleasing him.

Crossing the Finish Line

Have you come to the realization that we either dedicate our lives to pleasing ourselves or to pleasing God? Looking at your life, what is the ratio of building your kingdom to building God's? What changes should you make?

DAY TWENTY-FIVE

BLAZING A NEW TRAIL

Angela Ruth Strong

While Angela Ruth Strong's husband is the rider, she's the writer. Her romance novels have been adapted to film, won awards, and become Amazon bestsellers. Her next romantic comedy is based on her career as a flight attendant. Find out more at www.angelaruthstrong.com.

Every summer, my husband and I go on a couples' ride with friends to different national parks. In 2022, we headed to Glacier on our 2018 Street Glide Special. We were excited to arrive in Montana and had the whole trip in front of us. However, we ended up taking a much different vacation than planned.

Our group started the day by riding over Hungry Horse Dam on our way to downtown Whitefish for lunch. After our meal, we prepared to hop back on the Harleys.

My husband, Jim, climbed in the saddle and started our bike. I pulled on my helmet and waited for him to back up from the curb. Before he even moved, a man ran over.

"Your bike's on fire!" the guy yelled.

Jim gave him a thumbs up. "Thanks, man."

"No! Your bike's really on fire!"

That's when we noticed flames shooting out from underneath the saddle. Jim quickly put the kickstand down and climbed off. I ran inside the closest business in search of a fire extinguisher. A shop-keeper came to our rescue, putting out the flames.

The rest of our group joined us to troubleshoot the problem. They removed our saddle and started the bike a second time. Once again, the ignition coil caught fire from the fuel vape line. Stuck far from a Harley repair shop, and even farther from home, we had no bike to ride.

Thankfully, one of the other wives had driven a chaser vehicle. She offered to ride with her hubby on his bike and let us take her car. But we still didn't have a way to get our motorcycle home.

Over dinner, we considered options and decided to rent a U-Haul to drive the bike straight home. One of the other riders even offered us a stay in his cabin on the way to break up our trip. We thanked them and said our goodbyes.

I expected a somber drive back to Idaho because I knew my husband was bummed, but it turned into one of our best memories. We took our time, enjoyed the scenery, and made all the jokes.

At one point another U-Haul driver passed us, waving excitedly. We knew motorcyclists flash each other a motorcycle salute in passing, but we hadn't realized it was a U-Haul thing too. We laughed until we cried.

Two years later we returned to Glacier, with a special stop in Whitefish for a moment of silence.

Our bike could have caught fire while we were in the middle of nowhere. We might have been injured or at least stranded. God provided a stranger to warn us, a fire extinguisher to put out the flames, a vehicle to drive, and a beautiful mountain retreat on our unexpected detour. Though it's not how we would have planned our first trip to Glacier, we made the most of it and found many reasons to be grateful.

Daniel Boone blazed new trails by using his ax to knock off tree bark, leaving the white trunk to mark the trail. For Angela and Jim, they literally blazed a new trail to Glacier National Park, a stunning mecca for bikers with its Going to the Sun Road, and they completed that two years later.

What about blazing new trails for all of us? Frankly, people vary in their desire for security or new dimensions of life. Both have benefits and faults, but I suggest that new trails are vital for those who follow Jesus. Spiritual growth requires a dynamic life of changes, not a static one.

The first step brings not just a trail, but a new life: "We were therefore buried with him through baptism into death in order that, just as Christ was raised from the dead through the glory of the Father, we too may live *a new life*" (Romans 6:4). What an awesome image that our old person died, got planted, then, like Jesus, rose. But where do we go next?

Peter, in his second letter, blazed out our trail in following Jesus: ". . . *make every effort* to *add to* your faith goodness; and to goodness, knowledge; and to knowledge, self-control; and to self-control, perseverance; and to perseverance, godliness; and to godliness, mutual affection; and to mutual affection, love. For if you possess these qualities in increasing measure, they will *keep you from being ineffective and unproductive*" (1:5–8).

The goal comes at the end: We become effective and productive. We grow more solid in our connection with God. We become more effective in how we serve God and his kingdom. We blaze new trails that touch our behavior. We blaze new trails of character, the deeply embedded values that match God's character. We blaze new trails in serving him that seem beyond our abilities.

That first blaze beckons us to have faith in Jesus, but notice two factors in that first sentence. First, "make every effort." May we never consider faith to be easy: "And without faith it is impossible to please God, because anyone who comes to him must believe that he exists and that he rewards those who *earnestly seek* him" (Hebrews 11:6). Just as old Daniel endured difficulties in blazing his trails, so will we. The trail requires diligence.

Also notice the second factor in that first sentence: "add." We start with faith, then the adventure starts. Notice the progression: The first step leads to the second, which leads to the third, and on. A logical order, from one blaze to another.

Peter suggests that we can't hopscotch to the last blaze, which is agape, or unconditional love. We need some faith before goodness, although we won't be fully good. Some goodness brings some knowledge. But we follow the trail Peter blazed for us, and arrive safe and joyful.

Kick-Starting the Application

Look again at the order of the steps. Do you have some logjams that need clearing before moving along the trail? How can you remove them?

DAY TWENTY-SIX

NOT READY: A MESSAGE FROM LONG RIDES

For decades, music played little role on my long rides. My first two bikes, my 1970 Honda CL350 and 1973 CB 750, had neither fairing nor windscreen. Most bikes then didn't have the technology, or the wind drowned out the sound. For three years I did some listening with earbuds to Pandora on my 2003 Goldwing, combining Iz and worship music and classic rock, but to be frank, I loved the sounds of silence more than the distractions of other people's thoughts in music. Somehow, in our time jammed with activities and worry, we find it hard to meditate. Riding provided that.

Silence gave time to ponder, to examine my past and myself, both good and bad. Typically, conversations with God came along, asking for wisdom and an accurate memory. Listening for the soft whispers of his Spirit. Often the topic of why I made various choices came up. Why did my romantic relationships only last three months? Why did I not pursue some options for marriage, ones that sometimes came close? I always had jobs and paid the bills, but no women or jobs captivated me.

The silence of the road helped me realize two main things. First, romantically I wasn't ready to settle down into a long-term relationship. About three months in, the thrill of newness had eased off, and stability lost out to freedom. And frankly, at that time I subconsciously realized I wasn't a particularly good catch for anyone—too unstable, too unsettled, not ready to settle down. I didn't want to start a serious relationship when unwilling to let it develop where it might; that wouldn't be fair to the woman. A sacrificial act of kindness, perhaps?

Jobwise, no professional passion challenged my love of knocking on new doors. Several times my bosses wanted to move me into upper management or even to buy them out in time. Jobs I enjoyed but not to the level of giving my life to. The longest job in my 20s was two years teaching junior high in the inner city of Inglewood. In many ways I loved it, but the low pay and headaches each night from wrangling junior high schoolers wore me out.

The Eagles could have written their song "Desperado" about me.

Ironically, one of my greatest adventures, moving to Taos, brought me to a professional purpose worthy of giving my life to: pastoring and spiritually serving people. I found a church that loved me, used me, and showed what ministry could be. Yes, knowing the consequences required a lot of wrestling with God and some people in the church. He's gone now, but Dean Henbest was a godly thorn in my flesh.

That decision dominated my career from then on, even into official retirement. Ironically, that decision also led me away from Taos—Taos had served its purpose for me. This new stability brought the courage to enter a relationship, open to wherever it went. February 10, 2026, will mark 47 years of marriage . . . to a woman I met at that first ministry church.

Why this story of extended personal introspection? These books typically don't go in this direction of a captivating story and some application. But please use my story as a template. You will have different questions to figure out. You will have different personal issues than I faced. But take Socrates's wisdom to heart, with this line from his trial: "The unexamined life is not worth living." The point: We all need to have some margins in life. Spaces where we can think and ponder and wonder and pray. Where we can invite God in and ask some honest and deep questions about who we are.

Not all of you ride, and I get that. Long rides for me became a tool that almost forced me to examine myself. Find what works for you. But realize, examining ourselves and our walk with Jesus is a biblical command: "*Test yourselves* to make sure you are solid in the faith. Don't drift along taking everything for granted. Give yourselves *regular checkups*" (2 Corinthians 13:5 MSG).

For us to do this, we leave some time margins. Yes, life is costly and busy and we need to work, but perhaps we should pray about choosing to give ourselves enough quiet to ponder life. Ourselves. God. Decisions. And God, the ultimately wise Creator of the universe and us, gets our time crunch. To help us have the time to test ourselves and our faith.

God gave an example and a command to slow down: "*Work* six days and do everything you need to do. *But* the seventh day is a Sabbath to GOD, your God. *Don't do any work*. . . . For in six days GOD made Heaven, Earth, and sea, and everything in them; *he rested* on the seventh day. Therefore GOD blessed the Sabbath day; he set it apart as a holy day" (Exodus 20:8–11 MSG).

Whether we make it a day, usually Sunday now, or whatever, have we chosen a pace that leaves ample time to think more deeply? Do we gather enough courage to examine ourselves rigorously? Honestly, this process doesn't always bring joy. It does bring a greater sense of peace in life, the chance to grow beyond our previous problems. But these only arrive when we slow down, ponder, and listen.

Not long ago on Facebook, someone posted a poem by Max Ehrmann, "Desiderata," with the opening line, "*Go placidly* amid the noise and the haste, and remember what *peace there may be in silence*." I suspect we can go placidly amid the noise and haste when we slow down. We gain peace. We gain insights. We gain.

Kick-Starting the Application

Have you taken time to examine your life? Your good decisions and bad? Your strengths and weaknesses? Does your life allow time to go placidly amid the noise and haste? Do you allow busyness to drown out God's whispers? Do you need to make some lifestyle changes to allow silence?

DAY TWENTY-SEVEN

MODIFYING AN ALREADY NICE VETTE

Jerry Christensen

Jerry was born in Long Beach, California, a long time ago and later became a pastor, serving in Oregon, New Mexico, Oklahoma, and California. His love of riding began at around 10 years old, riding Cushman scooters on his aunt and uncle's grape farm. He's put a lot of miles on around 20 different bikes and still rides as often as Oregon weather allows.

Speed's Way

Over the years I've noticed that people really differ, which certainly adds spice to life. Some seem content with their lot in life, while others want to take what we have and kick it up a notch. Is one better or more spiritual than the other? You decide, but I clearly fall in the latter.

When young, I realized that I could improve things with just a few tweaks, often not involving much money. When I was about 10 or 11 years old, my parents gave me my first drum set, and when I added better cymbals and a foot pedal, that made it easier to play and completely changed the sound.

Every car required some aftermarket accessories: wheels, exhaust, paint, and so on. At 19, I bought a 1958 Corvette, a dream car for someone my age. But soon I started thinking about how to better it. Had it repainted, put in a new transmission, and, of course, got a new set of wheels.

It began as a beautiful car and I was content, but it became more cool and even better, at least in my mind. The joy that car brought was incredible. For two summers my motorcycle riding buddy Tim and I took it up to our church camp in the San Gabriel mountains. We had a blast driving the mountain roads with the top off, music loud, doing donuts in the dirt in front of the dining hall, and, more importantly, impressing every girl we met.

And that same attitude about making things better has continued with my 20 motorcycles, be it paint, phone holders, backrests, Bluetooth devices, or racks. Each of these improvements has made riding around the country easier and safer, allowing me to ride for over 60 years around the United States and Canada.

But more importantly, this drive to improve things has helped in my ministry life: seeing the good in others that they might not see in themselves, helping them stretch their faith, take on new challenges, even the courage to face the end of their lives.

However, like many good things, there is also a dark side for someone who is always trying to make things better: discontentment. Sometimes it's a fine line between trying to make something better and not being happy with what you have. In Philippians 4 the apostle Paul wrote, "I have learned to be content whatever the circumstances. . . . I have learned the secret of being content in any and every situation. . . . I can do all this through him who gives me strength" (verses 11–13).

If you also like to see things improve or help people live richer lives, make sure to act with grace. We can't change people, just influence them. And frankly, we all need some godly discontent to grow in our walk with Jesus, yet we need to balance that with honoring and celebrating the way God made us.

DAY TWENTY-SEVEN

God's Way

Jerry's story touches on two sometimes paradoxical qualities: ambition (the desire to improve) and contentment (the satisfaction with what we currently have). In prepping for this application, I researched all the New Testament verses on those two and was quite surprised.

Six verses mentioned content or contentment, all of which referred to the material stuff of life: food, shelter, clothing, pay (Luke 3:14; 1 Corinthians 7:21; Philippians 4:11–12; 1 Timothy 6:6, 8; Hebrews 13:5). Recall that Jerry used the Philippians verses. They all match.

God knows we need the stuff of life, and he doesn't desire that we cling to poverty. But only contentment with what we have allows us to slay the dragon of self-interest. On our own, we want stuff, more stuff. We see that in the growth of self-storage places, where our houses and garages can't contain all we've accumulated. The Old Testament word for that is *covet*, to want more. To want other's stuff.

Two different Greek words get translated as *content*: one suggests unfailing strength. It takes desire and work to gain contentment; it goes against the grain of our nature. The other has the hint of sufficiency. Knowing that if we have the basics, we have enough. We don't need to run after these things when we grasp, deep down, that this is sufficient.

Paul used that word in the verse Jerry used, and in the context, at various times he had plenty, other times was poor. Sometimes ate gourmet style; other times he dined on Spam. But all were sufficient. If you get more, great. If you don't, great. Would we like more? Often. Do we give our lives to getting more? Not necessarily. That's why the authors commanded contentment. Because that makes our lives better.

Yes, contentment has a downside, when it flows from laziness or irresponsibility. Being content with this motive doesn't qualify as godly.

In researching ambition, six more nuggets came up. Again, two different Greek words were used; they divide ambition into good and bad categories. One word produces two English words: selfish ambition (Galatians 5:20; Philippians 1:17, 23; James 3:14, 16). This ambition considers our needs and desires as paramount. We don't factor in the damage that might bring to others; we care little about their needs. That contradicts the very nature of Jesus, who came to serve. Selfish ambition wants others to serve us.

But ambition possesses an exceptionally godly dimension, like Paul possessed: "It has always been *my ambition* to preach the gospel where Christ was not known" (Romans 15:20). That word for ambition means to strive, to put energy into the goal of reaching people for Jesus.

Selfish ambition destroys the godly life: "For where you have envy and selfish ambition, there you find disorder and every evil practice" (James 3:16).

How do we blend contentment and ambition? We choose to say that what we have is sufficient and strive to serve God and grow in godliness.

Crossing The Finishing Line

Do you have spiritual ambitions or just kind of float through? Are you striving to get closer? Do you have a basic sense of sufficiency in what life situation and stuff you now have? Do you strive for stuff to the degree that it damages others or your spiritual life?

DAY TWENTY-EIGHT

JUST RIDE

Jody Shorkey

Jody Shorkey is the senior pastor of Lincoln Community Church in Lincoln, California. As a teenager, he learned to ride motorcycles in the deserts of Southern California with his family. He understood early in life that a little sand in your seat was not always a bad thing.

It was September 2015, and my 10-year-old Suzuki M109 and I had not been on a multistate ride for a while. So I decided that leaving northern California and heading for Oregon, Idaho, Utah, Nevada, and Arizona and back to California was a great idea. My wife agreed and sent me on my way.

Every motorcycle rider always wants certain things: a full gas tank, smooth roads, and good weather. Of course, life often presents unexpected conditions that prevent us from getting exactly what we hoped for.

I arrived in Oregon on my first day to meet rain as I pulled into the hotel where I spent the night. However, looking at the weather report for the next day, the predictions said no rain, so I concluded that was a good thing. When I awoke and looked out the window, the sun shone, and the sky was a bright blue without a cloud. *Good for me!* I thought.

DAY TWENTY-EIGHT

Everything was working out just as I had hoped it would that morning. I packed my gear to get ready for the 300-mile ride to Idaho. I left my things in the room and walked outside to the kitchen to get some breakfast, and that is when I learned something about Oregon.

In Oregon, sunshine and clear blue skies do not mean the same thing as they do in California. It was a bone-chilling 36 degrees outside my hotel door.

My hands nearly froze as I walked downstairs, and I no longer thought about breakfast but about riding my motorcycle in such cold weather.

I grabbed a hot chocolate and an apple and stood inside the warm kitchen, looking out the window at my motorcycle. I knew that my bike wanted to go to Idaho, but I wanted to think about it and weigh my options.

After such a nutritious meal, I could not ignore my fate. I went to my room, prayed for a good ride, packed my T-bag, grabbed my helmet and gloves, and said, "Just ride!"

I marched to my motorcycle, loaded my gear, and put on my helmet and gloves. But for the first time in my 50-plus years of riding, I dreaded getting on my motorcycle.

I advised myself once more, "Just ride." When I started the motorcycle and listened to the engine come to life, I felt an excitement I had not felt all morning.

As I pulled out of the driveway going north, I did what every motorcycle rider does: I leaned to the right, and the motorcycle naturally followed my lead and turned right. "Good for me!"

The cold no longer concerned me. I was riding!

In all my motorcycle seasons, I can honestly say that my trip from Lakeview, Oregon, to Boise, Idaho, will always be one of my top three rides. Thank you, God.

DAY TWENTY-EIGHT

How do we decide to "just ride?" Do we get a wild hair and take off? Or do we do our homework first, like Jody? Prep the bike, figure out a route? Jody gives us a pattern for all the spiritual decisions we face: Accepting Jesus as Savior and Lord. A major step in following him, maybe a ministry. Buying a house. Marrying someone. God gives us some tips on making those decisions, so we can just ride and experience the best of life.

Here's why we need to factor in reason: Jesus is called the Word in John 1:1. The Greek is *logos*, encompassing reason. Logic. Thinking. These must play a role in deciding tough questions. So how do we scripturally use logic on our decisions?

In John 1:38–46, twice the phrase "Come and see" was said to people who had some interest in learning about Jesus. Jesus used it first to two of John the Baptizer's followers, then Phillip said it to an interested Nathaniel (verses 39 and 46). Check it out for yourself. Experience Jesus. We don't make such a momentous decision as following Jesus on blind faith but on informed faith. Don't take another's words as absolute truth, but we research it ourselves.

In Luke 14, Jesus cautioned people about following: "Suppose one of you wants to build a tower. Won't you first sit down and *estimate the cost* to see if you have enough money to complete it? For if you lay the foundation and are not able to finish it, everyone who sees it will ridicule you" (verses 28–29). Jesus wanted people to follow him but on an informed and calculated basis. Not on blind faith, not on emotion.

He wants us to explore the evidence. The historicity of Jesus. The degree of commitment when we accept Jesus as Lord. Don't just jump into the water without checking out the warmth and depth.

I've seen many who made a quick and emotional decision for Jesus, and it seems like those who take the time and research the evidence stick around longer and grow stronger. Emotions ebb and flow, and if they build our primary foundation, we may have a shaky faith. I suspect this strategy applies to all of our life decisions.

For me, I accepted Christ early and sincerely but shallowly. College caused me to realize that my faith came from others, so I began a three-year exploration of world religions, open to wherever it led me. Christianity and the God of the Bible seemed the most logical, but it didn't quite get me there. So one night I prayed, "God, I think you're likely real. I need to make some changes, and I give you permission to do that."

Did I know that would work? I wasn't sure, but I tested him, and he came through. So yes, a bit of a leap of faith. Now, I just ride through life, with a solid foundation. I hope you share that.

Kick-Starting the Application

If you already follow Jesus, how did reason and emotion balance when you came to Christ? If you're not yet a follower, does this Day impact you? Overall, where do you land making most decisions? What's behind that history? How can you find a better balance, so you can just ride with God through life?

DAY TWENTY-NINE

DON'T LOOK WHERE YOU DON'T WANT TO GO

Doug Cole

Doug grew up in Colorado, went to school in West Texas, married the love of his life in '78, moved to California in '79, and has served full-time in the Lord's church since then. He loves the outdoors and the freedom of an open road, but more than anything, he is constantly amazed that the Almighty God loves him.

Mike grew up in Oklahoma, and after spending about 30 years in Southern California, he was ready to head home. We had often ridden together and wanted to do one last ride. Being accomplished riders, we chose some of the twistiest roads to challenge our skills and provide that adrenaline rush they provide. One road, the South Grade up Palomar Mountain, even made the top 50 of the most technical rides in the United States.

Rules and rhythms must be followed when driving motorcycles through the twists and turns, and when they become tighter and follow one after another, those rules and rhythms grow in importance. Riders consider lane position when entering and exiting a turn, must be aware of speed and braking and how both affect traction, and if the front or rear brake should be used for different parts of the turn.

DAY TWENTY-NINE

Riders also deal with changing road conditions, like gravel or sand or uneven asphalt that could interrupt a smooth transition in the turn, and they must make the correct adjustments. But maybe the most important rule of riding a motorcycle is to always look where you want to go.

We had just finished one of the most challenging sections, diving in and out of hairpin switchbacks and curves, which tested all of our skills. Enjoying the power of our motorcycles, we quickly accelerated out of each turn and prepared to dive into the next, but now we had popped out on top: a time to relax and enjoy the scenery.

Such a beautiful day to ride, with the sun shining amid blue sky, with lush green fields and orchards below. A smile spread across my face as I breathed deep and took in the beauty around me, but in my comfort, I forgot that one foundational rule of riding a motorcycle, and before I knew it, death stared me in the face.

Then came the easy part of the road, relaxing as we approached a gentle sweeping left-hand curve, I looked sideways too long at the valley below and began to drift that way. I still remember every detail of the edge of that road, scattered with loose gravel, and then the drop-off next to it. Scenarios of what could happen rapidly filled my brain, and none looked good.

The adrenaline surged through my veins, but I kept my focus on the edge of the road. I should have been able to easily steer away from the danger, but as I focused on the edge, the motorcycle absolutely refused to respond to my urgent wish to return to safety on the pavement.

Just before the motorcycle and I made a sliding exit into oblivion, the road straightened.

The day remained beautiful, although I did have to stop and catch my breath. It still surprises me that it was so hard to look away from what I dreaded and how insistent the motorcycle was to follow my line of sight.

DAY TWENTY-NINE

Yep, a basic rule of riding: You go where you look, because whether on a bike or sports car, our body instinctively makes the necessary movements to follow our eyes. And when Doug forgot that, he almost flew off the mountain road.

That principle also applies to following Jesus: When we fill our lives with things of the flesh, our sinful human nature, we head in that direction. When we fill our lives with things of the Spirit, we head that way: "Those who live according to the flesh have *their minds set on what the flesh desires*; but those who live in accordance with the Spirit have *their minds set on what the Spirit desires*. The mind governed by the flesh is death, but the mind governed by the Spirit is life and peace" (Romans 8:5–6).

Paul says we should choose our preferred destination and fix our eyes, or set our minds, on that. But in practical terms, what does it mean to set our minds on spiritual things? How do we fill our minds and lives with the Spirit? Paul wrote, "*Be filled with the Spirit, speaking* to one another in psalms and hymns and spiritual songs, *singing and making* melody in your heart to the Lord, *giving thanks* always for all things to God the Father in the name of our Lord Jesus Christ, *submitting* to one another in the fear of God" (Ephesians 5:18–21 NKJV).

Paul commands that we actively *choose* being filled with the Spirit, then he gives five participles (verbs ending with *-ing* that modify a noun—here, filled with the Spirit). Those five describe how to let the Spirit fill us. Or, how we fix our eyes on Jesus, our destination (Hebrews 12:1–2). My pastor, Chris Brown of North Coast Church of Vista, California, phrases it, "we hang out where the Spirit hangs out.

We speak to one another about God stuff. We talk to fellow followers about the goodness and to those not yet followers when appropriate. We sing praise directly to God. I often use the Mercy Me site on Pandora and sing along. We give thanks, recognizing that all good gifts come from God (James 1:17). And we submit to each other: "Each of you should look not only to your *own interests*, but also to the *interests of others*" (Philippians 2:4 BSB). We transcend our self-centeredness.

These five allow us to fix our eyes on where we want to go. Obviously, if we choose to fill our lives with thoughts and actions that flow from our sinful nature, our lives gravitate in that direction. Notice that the Spirit doesn't fill us by his actions; we do it by ours.

So one final word. Where are you looking? What fills your life?

Kick-Starting the Application

How well do you intentionally fix your eyes on the spiritual life? Do you have some areas where you focus too much on the sinful nature? What can you do this week to better focus on the Spirit?

DAY THIRTY

BEAUTY AND VARIETY

Last May I gained a lesson because of one of the most boring stretches of road I've ever been on. The trip had already brought some troubles. My new tires turned out to be improperly balanced, which caused a significant shimmy on the Utah part of the ride. A shop in Ogden fixed it but overcharged me significantly. You can read about that in Day 33, "Stand Up for . . . Justice." Then rain and snow and low temps kept us from our primary target: the central mountains of Idaho. Sorry, no Day on that.

We had some great times exploring Shoshone Falls in Twin Falls, Idaho. They look stupendous when in full flow, wide and high with a variety of channels carved by the Snake River. However, the two times I've been here, part of the river was diverted or low. Still worth the drive, and I would do it again. Best of all, I had a fine time at dinner at a German restaurant with my grandson Josh and his wife Kate in Meridian, Idaho.

Then came the time to head home, so Jerry and I left Meridian at about 8:00 in the morning, fleeing the sun on I-84. Nice riding weather, a welcomed change. Near Ontario, Oregon, we jumped on Highway 20 and west to John Day, Oregon, where we split. He continued west to Bend and Sisters to his home near Salem, as I turned south on Highway 395 toward my Temecula abode. He had the best route.

DAY THIRTY

To be brief, much of 395 in that part of Oregon consists of boring brush. Blah scenery. Mostly straight roads. The bike didn't match my previous Goldwing for wind protection at 80 miles per hour, so music wasn't an option. I did outline some *Unconventional* posts in my mind to write down that evening, like this one. But I got bored and tired and a bit sleepy with little to draw and keep my attention. Okay, sleepy enough to genuinely concern me.

Then I saw a sign for Poverty Basin a few miles ahead and hoped for a gas station with cold drinks and snacks with another seat to sit on for a while. Instead, I saw just a small dirt road heading west, with nothing but a weathered sign with an arrow west to Poverty Basin. But I pulled onto the dirt, walked around and threw a few rocks and stretched to bring back some ability to focus before returning to boredom on 395. About the time tiredness resurrected, I entered a gorgeous 20-mile valley with lakes and a river and curves . . . blessed curves!

That variety got me to Lakeview, my stop for the night in a clean motel. Yes, it needed some upkeep outside—pretty plain and barren. No breakfast, no lobby. The basic room had a good bed and a fine shower. Downtown I found a historic bank converted into a restaurant; all of this restored me, ready to ride again. Then, in the restaurant, while waiting for my beer and burger to be served, the lesson arrived.

The key to safe rides on a bike, through life, or with Jesus: Avoid boredom. We need to stay active and engaged in the world around us. In thinking about this topic, an old saying came to mind, which came from The Living Bible's paraphrase, "Idle hands are the devil's workshop." I suspect boredom also leads to idle hands. Some time back soft porn caught me and in my recovery groups I came across the acronym HALT to describe vulnerability for any sin: Hungry, Angry, Lonely, Tired.

For me the greatest vulnerability comes from boredom, like I experienced on that blah Oregon road. Nothing caught my attention.

No surrounding beauty. No surrounding variety, just flat scrub. Little activity, just keeping the bike pointed straight ahead.

The apostles seemed to have faced that. After Jesus's resurrection but before his ascension and Pentecost, he commanded, "Do not leave Jerusalem, but wait for the gift my Father promised" (Acts 1:4). But with nothing to do but wait, it seems they got bored and not only left Jerusalem but returned to Galilee. Peter again took the lead, "'I'm going out to fish,' . . . and they said, 'We'll go with you'" (John 21:3).

Boredom leads to disobedience. Sleepiness. Inactivity. But boredom can create motivation—to find healthy activity, maybe prayer. Once we realize the danger that boredom brings, we craft a strategy to stave it off. Here are a few tips.

First, stay active. Yes, we need rest; we need quiet times to meditate. But the apostles' disobedience came from having little to do but wait. My ministry mentor, Herb Read, gave the staff a weekly calendar with the days on a large column on the left, on the top right a list of tasks for the week, and at the bottom right a prayer list. That was in 1978, and 47 years later in retirement, I still use it. If you'd like a digital template, just email me.

Second, stay mental: "Whatever is true, whatever is noble, whatever is right, whatever is pure, whatever is lovely, whatever is admirable—if anything is excellent or praiseworthy—think about such things. . . . And the God of peace will be with you" (Philippians 4:8–9). We look for and think about the beauty God places in life. We change things up; many things "come to pass, not to stay." One saving grace on that ride on 395 came from thinking about what I could learn, and this Day came from that.

So we fill our lives with beauty and variety to keep us attentive. We fill our minds with God thoughts, to take on new challenges. I suppose the apostles' boredom disappeared on Pentecost, with a mission that captivated them. Yes, we can be too busy, but let's not be too inactive either.

Kick-Starting the Application

Does HALT or boredom increase your vulnerability? Which hits you the most? Have you built a strategy of looking for beauty and variety to add zest to your life and stave off boredom? How can you craft a strategy for a healthy level of interactivity with life?

DAY THIRTY-ONE

A DREAM OF SPEED

Karl Smith

Karl is an architect, a transportation designer and researcher, and a journalist living in Thousand Oaks, California. Fascinated by both the past and the future of the car, he has written extensively about both. He and his wife Leilani share a love of art, music, and travel.

Speed's Way

We had planned to rent a sports car and race along the famous Autobahn, with no speed limits, but the reality was quite different. It started at the airport car rental counter, where we got the first bad news: No sports cars available.

"But, we have a nice sports sedan for you, Mr. Smith."

OK, I thought, envisioning a nice BMW 3-series. That could work. Not as fun as a sports car, but it's something. But no. We were handed the keys to a Mercedes C class sedan. A fine car, but not the Ultimate Driving Machine. We soldiered on. The Mercedes was a nice car, just not the speedster we had hoped for.

A few days later, we headed out to see Cologne, Germany. This meant driving the Autobahn 50 miles from Aachen to Cologne. I looked forward to putting the Mercedes through its paces. We merged onto the Autobahn and prepared to make the jump to lightspeed when

. . . a speed limit sign! Construction ahead caused us to crawl along at 50 miles per hour. Ugh.

And more construction awaited us down the road, virtually all the way to Cologne. I don't think we ever got over 70 miles per hour. No matter, I set my hopes on the return drive and we had a great day walking through Cologne.

Unfortunately, we fared no better on the return trip. The crews had gone for the day, but barriers and equipment were still around, and the *Polizei* were still monitoring speeds. Such a disappointment.

But my dream of speed was resurrected a few days later, when we boarded a train from Brussels to London. We took the Eurostar, the high-speed train. We sat in comfort and in great anticipation of the ride. At last, no disappointment! The train's speed rose rapidly as we kept watch on the speedometer mounted on the ceiling. Passing from Belgium to France, we watched the speed rise from 72 miles per hour to 90 to 120 to 145, going faster and faster as we streaked through the French countryside.

Finally, the Eurostar peaked at 280 kilometers per hour, just short of its maximum speed of 300. Two hundred and eighty kilometers per hour—that's 174 miles per hour! The fastest I have ever traveled on land. The world outside was blur; entire cities zipped by in a flash.

Flying home 10 days later, I thought about Proverbs 16:9 (NKJV): "A man's heart plans his way, But the Lord directs his steps."

I had dreamed a dream of speed, blasting down the Autobahn, setting a personal land speed record. God had other plans—a faster speed but in other, more competent hands. God sometimes grants our wishes, helps us realize our dreams. Other times he says no. And other times, he answers in ways we could never foresee.

We must be open to God's path in our lives, even if it looks totally different from what we imagined. Stay humble. Be ready. God will be there.

DAY THIRTY-ONE

God's Way

For those of us addicted to bikes or sports cars, a love of speed seems embedded in us, like it is in Karl. We love raw speed or precise cornering, the adrenaline rush when the speedometer increases. Jerry and I share a bike trip goal, to slip past 100 miles per hour at least once. On my Iron Butt ride at 70, on a lonely and straight Montana interstate, I still visualize the needle creeping past 100, then 110, soon 120, and finally 130 before I backed off to a safer 95 to 110 for two hours. One of the most thrilling episodes I've had.

So I could feel Karl's disappointment at the seven steps that curtailed his dream of speed on the Autobahn. But let's go beyond dreams of speed that get shafted to other dreams that get the same result. Another day explored when hopes and expectations get shattered, but dreams seem to dig their way deeper into our soul. Dreams touch on lifetime goals and worm their way into our existence and identity. Bucket lists may pale in comparison to dreams. Those lists are nice, but dreams touch our essence.

So let's go back to a thrilling day of yesteryear—like, thousands—to a man who realized our typical lifetime dreams. A fine marriage, great children, popular acclaim, and fantastic wealth. Successful, and I'm sure he dreamed of that continuing. We know him as Job, a man so righteous that God bragged about him. Satan said of course, you give him everything. So step by step, Satan took away Job's donkeys and their herders, his sheep and their shepherds, his camels and their jockeys, and finally the house collapsed, killing his children.

Then he broke out in painful sores, so bad his wife encouraged him to curse God so God would put him out of his misery. Yes, he felt the loss: "My days have passed, my plans are shattered" (Job 17:11). But I suspect he found dreams that transcended the material that allowed him to maintain his faithfulness: "God might kill me, but I have no other hope" (Job 13:15 NLT). Why? Job found a dream that transcended the more shallow dreams many of us possess: speed, a spouse, success, or we can fill in the blank.

The sneakiest verse in the Bible came in the next book: "Delight yourself in the LORD and he will give you the *desires of your heart*" (Psalm 37:4 ESV). Why sneaky? When we take delight in God, that tender connection that touches every layer of our being, our dreams and desires change. If we have nothing else, like Job, we have contentment. Why? We know the awesome Creator of the universe who knows us and loves us and lives in us. That dream can always be realized.

Crossing the Finish Line

What dreams do you have? Does knowing God rank high enough as a dream? What keeps you from more fully delighting in God? How can you increase that delight?

DAY THIRTY-TWO

CARS DIFFER

Speed's Way

On my Exotics adventure, the Lambo had to be my natural choice. My first college roommate, Ron Stump, put up a poster on our dorm wall of the current Lamborghini GT350, and that hooked me. Such a blend of streamlined and strength. Sheer artistry. This kid could dream, and I followed their evolution: Miura, Countach (one of my favorites), the Diablo and Murcielago.

The Indy cars then caught most of my attention, but when my hometown started the Long Beach Grand Prix, the Formula 1 road courses captivated me. I'd driven on most of those streets.

Several dreams converged on buying some laps on a road course with a supercar. That thrilled me, and my interest in Lambos grew. If I ever hit the lottery . . .

Upon pulling into the pits, Megan and I debriefed. Each lap was faster than the previous. I did pass a more powerful Lambo with a younger driver. And what-if thoughts slipped in. Then I asked Megan about her favorite car of all at the track. Immediately she smiled and said, "The Porsche GT3."

This Lambo lover had to ask why, and she replied, "It's a driver's car. I feel more at home in it." As she described it, her choice made sense. The Gallardo 550 was a big car, powerful, and it took work to maximize it. The smaller GT3 handled much better, especially on a road course. Well, that intrigued me, and I researched some of the differences between the two.

The Lambo slightly edges the GT in top speed, 201 to 197. Honestly, that makes little difference . . . just bragging rights. But the Lambo has more power, a 5.2-liter mid-engine V-10 producing 550 horses with its all-wheel drive. The GT3 offers a 3.8-liter rear-mounted flat six engine that gives 472 horses to its rear-wheel drive. The power-to-weight ratio favors the Lambo, at 0.156 horses per pound; the GT3 is 0.144. But the GT3 wins on weight, just 3,270 pounds to the Gallardo's 3,520.

Those differences affect how the cars handle. The Gallardo's "relentless pursuit of power" gives it the edge on the straights, but it can spin out if you accelerate too much too soon coming out of a turn. The GT3's lighter weight corners like it's on rails; one driver said you had to do something really stupid to cause the Porsche to spin out.

So which is best? Personal choice. For me, on an oval track with banked turns, I'd take the Lambo, but on a road course, I'd slip the Porsche into gear. A post on *Unconventional* talked about speed, and a sports car guy, Wayne Kempton, said, "Thanks to one of my previous careers (federal law enforcement agent), I have done more than enough high-speed driving in bygone years. Give me an agile sports car and a curvy canyon road and I am happy without going, as they say in my native New England, 'wicked fast.'"

Yes, the cars differ. But both are supercars.

God's Way

Think of that last sentence as a metaphor for believers. This passage took my understanding of following Jesus from the level of a Honda Accord to a Lamborghini Gallardo. I pray it may have a similar impact on you: "And He Himself gave *some* to be *apostles, some prophets, some evangelists, and some pastors and teachers*, for the *equipping of the saints for the work of ministry*, for the edifying of the body of

Christ, till *we all* come to the unity of the faith and of the knowledge of the Son of God, to a perfect man, to the measure of the stature of the *fullness of Christ*" (Ephesians 4:11–13 NKJV)

Let's pull out some nuggets. The Exotics cars each differed, yet all were supercars, just like us. Look at the differences between followers of Jesus in the text above, and let me geek out a bit on word choice and repetition.

Regarding leaders, in verse 11 Paul used the adjective *some* in italics for each group—apostles, prophets, evangelists, pastors, and teachers. Clearly, not all followers are leaders. Just some have been given leadership abilities. Then, Paul addressed the greater body of Christ, again in italics in verse 13, "*we all.*" We all differ, and we'll circle back to this in a moment.

Here's an acronym I stole from Rick Warren to delve deeper into our differences. We all have a different SHAPE: our Spiritual gifts, our Heart that drives us, our Abilities we were born with or developed, our Personality unique to us, and our Experiences. Not one else in all creation can match our SHAPE, and our unique SHAPE drives how we minister.

We have no need to envy others, nor to compare. No one can do the kingdom work that we can. So we rejoice in our differences.

But our uniqueness changes how we run our races. Go back to verse 11 and notice the differing roles: Leaders serve the greater body by equipping them to better minister. We all serve as ministers who serve to grow the body of Christ.

Going back to our metaphor: What makes us supercars, or effective ministers? Do we run our race, using our SHAPE to the best of our abilities as God empowers us? "Each of you *should use whatever gift you have received* to serve others, as faithful stewards of God's grace in its various forms" (1 Peter 4:10).

A supercar never uses its abilities if it stays garaged. So in effect, it's not functionally a supercar then. What a sad oxymoron when the church's servants—us—don't serve.

Gallardos and GT3s differ as supercars, as do followers of Jesus. Our super servant status flows from being in the race and crossing our finish line: reaching the fullness of Christ.

Crossing the Finish Line

Have you ever considered yourself as a supercar of faith? Do you see how simple it is to be one? How can you up your game in the race of following Jesus?

DAY THIRTY-THREE

STAND UP FOR . . . JUSTICE

Knowing the odds, I knew this 2024 ride to Idaho could likely be Jerry's and my last long ride together, so we both wanted to maximize what could be the culmination of over 50 years of riding together. The goal: Idaho's central mountains. We planned our routes for one solo night for each before meeting in Ogden, Utah. Then we'd cruise together north into Idaho, then ride west to John Day, Oregon, where we'd split off. And we both made sure our bikes were ready.

My tires wouldn't last the projected 3,000 miles, so I took it to the Honda shop for new tires and balancing and new 90-degree valve stems. The close quarters of the back tire stem made it hard to reach. Sadly, when they brought the bike out, the stems pointed to the left side, and I had asked for the right. If you ride, you understand. That should have sounded a warning, but they apologized and quickly fixed it; I took it on our local freeway, up to maybe 72, and it ran smoothly. One happy biker, ready for an epic last ride.

Until I passed St. George on I-15. The speed limit increased to 80, with traffic flow exceeding that, so I matched them. At 75, I felt a slight shimmy. Not bad, but not right. Hitting 80 the shimmy turned into a minor wobble, and if I exceeded that, the wobble got big. Scary big. So I slowly cruised to Richfield for the night, then to Ogden the next day. A local Honda dealer had my tire in stock and could fit me in the next morning. We rode there and asked them to check the balance and, if it was okay, to then diagnose the issue.

Their estimate: $562 just to balance the tire. I questioned that but they wouldn't budge, and I was a stuck on the road and couldn't continue with that death wobble, so I agreed. They found way too many balancing weights, almost placed at random. They fixed it, so I smiled and said thanks, but I remained unhappy about my local dealer for not doing an easy job and at this Honda dealer for dishonesty. By the way, that Ogden dealer was neither Newgate nor Monarch. 'Nuff said.

Upon my return, I rode over and talked to the manager at my local shop and shared the situation. After some negotiating and discussion, he agreed to "make it right." His normal cost to balance tires was only $90, not $562. He called the Ogden shop about the high bill; they wouldn't call back. So I filed a fraud claim with the credit card company and called the Ogden shop who surprisingly responded. After more discussion they more than cut the bill in half, and my local guy covered the rest. If you're in southwest Riverside County, California, I heartily recommend the folks at Temecula Powersports. They make mistakes, but they make it right.

And I learned a lesson: Justice is good. Accountability is important. And sometimes we need to take some effort to reach it.

Some followers dislike Christians going to court for legal issues because of Paul's advice in his first letter to the Corinthian church in 6:1–8. Verse 1 says, "If any of you has a *dispute with another*, do you dare to take it before the ungodly for judgment instead of before the Lord's people?" But when Paul said this, he referred to believers taking other believers to court, not to all law suits. Notice the "dispute with one another." He doesn't allow mistreatment, and this only tells believers not to sue one another but to let the church judge the matter.

God values justice, that all of his human creation be treated fairly, that their property rights be respected. I first called this Day "Stand Up for Yourselves," but the deeper issue is justice. Fair treatment. If a person is wronged, they're entitled to fair compensation for their loss. Wade through Exodus, Leviticus, and Deuteronomy, and notice the detailed commands to enforce justice. Here's one example from

Exodus 21:18–19: "If people quarrel and one person hits another with a stone or with their fist and the victim does not die but is confined to bed, the one who struck the blow will not be held liable if the other can get up and walk around outside with a staff; however, the guilty party must pay the injured person for any loss of time and see that the victim is *completely healed*."

Paul himself used the legal system to his advantage. Born a Roman citizen, Paul used that status legally. In Acts he journeyed to Jerusalem and annoyed the Jewish leaders enough to have him arrested, and when a riot broke out a Roman commander ordered he be flogged. Paul turned to a centurion and asked, "Is it legal for you to flog a Roman citizen who hasn't even been found guilty?" (Acts 22:25). The centurion was at risk for violating the rights of a citizen. He quickly changed the tune, then a trial began with the Romans and Jews, and once more knowing legal rights, Paul appealed to Caesar, the right of all Roman citizens (25:11–12). Paul wouldn't violate his own words so lightly. Ironically, that also allowed Paul an all-expenses-paid cruise to Rome to talk to Caesar.

The need for justice flows from the innate worth of every human whom God loves. But if we ignore bad behavior, the perpetrator learns they can get away with it and cheat more people. We increase the evil in the world. The legal system is our instrument of justice, of fair treatment for all, on telling bad actors that's not acceptable.

The meaning for us: God cares about justice. For us, for all. Maybe we can incorporate that into our lives.

Kick-Starting the Application

How much concern do you have that all be treated fairly? Do you limit your justice to those you like? How can knowing justice is God's heart affect your life?

DAY THIRTY-FOUR

A SPORTS CAR KINDA GUY—KINDA

Donald Patterson

Donald Patterson is a native Southern Californian, now pastoring in Missouri. He has dabbled in cartoons, articles, and fiction.

Speed's Way

Most guys would tear their tongues out before confessing this: I am not a sports car guy. Oh, I have the disease; it's in my blood. But I'm a carrier, not a casualty. I was inoculated young and often throughout my childhood. You see, my dad really was a bona fide car guy—not your average garden variety, either. He was a drag-racing, street-rod, sports car, do-it-yourself custom car guy. His '31 Model A Ford appeared on the covers of *Car Craft* and *Hot Rod* magazines. He once took first place over 2,000 other show cars. He even became 1989's Street-Rodder of the Year.

Me? Not so much.

I began to notice my affliction in high school. Things just weren't adding up. Several of my friends owned sporty Triumphs, TR-3s, and Sprites. I usually ended up riding on the skimpy luggage rack behind the seats, all six-foot-one of me. Of course, many had lame cars too—Ramblers, Metropolitans, the uglier Dodges. To my horror, I realized they were all uncool. Was I becoming a nerd?

My dad owned a Shelby Mustang, a Plymouth Roadrunner, and a hot four-speed Corvair Spyder, none of which I was allowed to drive. Instead, I occasionally drove my mom's Corvair Monza. The most embarrassing thing about the Monza was the gear lever. It did not have a racy four-on-the-floor, nor even a more pedestrian three-on-the-tree. No, it boasted an automatic transmission with a pathetic little lever sticking out of the dashboard next to the ignition switch. It reminded me of the handle of a spoon that I clicked up and down to select gears. I couldn't win.

The first car I bought with my own money was a 10-year-old Ford Town and Country station wagon. It threw a rod the day after I bought it. I went off to college with a wheezing 1960 Dodge Dart, the bulk of a Cadillac with a lousy straight six under the hood. Later, as a wedding present, my father-in-law gifted us what he promised was a "sports car." It turned out to be a Chevy Vega . . . Wagon.

Over the years, I've learned a few things about myself. Though I can appreciate speed and flash, I'm really more of a bread-and-butter kind of guy. The hottest car I've ever owned was a Honda Accord coupe. It's tough being the son of a gifted man. Thankfully, I have not spent my life trying to outdo him. I will forever be in his shadow, but I feel nothing but pride. I've found that I am quite good at other pursuits—art, writing, and woodworking. I may not be an automotive genius, but I am my father's son.

Oh, that Corvair Monza? Once in high school I gave a pretty girl a ride home. She eagerly flounced onto the passenger seat. As I sat down behind the wheel, she announced, "I just love sports cars."

"Yeah," I sighed. "Me too."

DAY THIRTY-FOUR

God's Way

Don recognized the unique giftedness of his dad and that he himself didn't share it. Many times, we sons admire our dads, desire to emulate them, and fail. Don realized both his dad's gifts and his lack in that area . . . but he had his own. When this biker devo series added sports cars, I first contacted Don. I'd read his stuff; now you can.

Don brings up an issue that we all face, whether we ride or have sports cars. How do we build our identity and self-worth? How do we gain affirmation from others in a healthy manner? Competing emerged as my early and unhealthy go-to trait to gain self-worth. I gained worth if I did something better than the other person. Of course, they remained oblivious to the competition; they just realized spending time with Tim didn't work well.

Then I found a verse that transformed my life: "Outdo one another in showing honor" (Romans 12:10 RSV). That's biblical competition—be the best at lifting others up, not putting them down. About that time, I came across a line in Max Ehrmann's "Desiderata": "If you compare yourself with others, you may become vain or bitter, for always there will be greater and lesser persons than yourself."

Paul examined that several times in his letter to the Corinthians, a church plagued by comparison and division. Some thought Paul was the best leader; others said Paul compared unfavorably to Apollos. Paul squelched that, saying that only God mattered: "For when one says, 'I follow Paul,' and another, 'I follow Apollos,' are you not mere human beings? What, after all, is Apollos? And what is Paul? Only servants, through whom you came to believe—as the Lord has assigned to each his task. I planted the seed, Apollos watered it, but God has been making it grow. So neither the one who plants nor the one who waters is anything, but only God, who makes things grow" (1 Corinthians 3:4–7).

He had to revisit that in 2 Corinthians about avoiding comparisons, in verses 12–28. The problem comes from how comparing takes our mind off God and puts it on people.

Since comparing to build identity doesn't work, what does? By doing our best job at being the unique person God designed us to be. Don recognized his own skill sets that gave the foundation for the unique person of God he is, which led to how he would serve God. Rick Warren suggested we each have a unique SHAPE, one only for us, much like our DNA.

Our Spiritual gifts enable us to serve: We all have some, and they seem to change through the years.

Our Heart: What moves us? What touches our emotions?

Our Abilities: Like Don's art, woodworking, and writing: That empowers our ministry.

Our Personality: It is totally unique to us and guides how we serve.

Our Experiences: These also are totally unique to us, and we add to them continually.

So we build identity and self-worth based on how we develop our SHAPE, in trying to serve and please him. God didn't make duplicates.

Crossing the Finish Line

How have you built your identity and self-worth? How has that worked? What makes you totally unique in God's eyes? How can you incorporate that as you serve him?

DAY THIRTY-FIVE

CHANGED PLANS: STRESS OR RELAX?

Back in 2022, Jerry and I made an audacious attempt: an 8,000-mile ride to the East Coast to get 22 more states on a bike for Jerry to total 48, and my last 3 to get all 50. Audacious, for two old guys in our mid-70s, but "hope lies eternal in the human breast." Gotta be crazy to ride anyway. We met in the Rockies and rode to the Midwest and Southeast, where I bagged my last 3 of 50, then up to Connecticut. That's where it all came apart. Jerry's Can Am crapped out getting on a freeway, and my Goldwing got totaled in trying to get back to him.

But we didn't give up the goal for Jerry, so we planned a 2023 ride to finish his states. The easternmost that counted would be Rhode Island, next go north up to Maine, then home across lower New England and the Upper Midwest. Jerry's back felt bad when he left his Oregon home on his first day, but he gave it a chance and got to Mountain Home, Idaho, when his back got so bad he had to return. Trip off.

After a few days it seemed improved, so he suggested I ride from SoCal to Oregon and we could make short day trips, always within a day of his home in case his back got wonky again. His back held together enough to attempt a multiday ride, go from Salem northeast on backroads to Estacada and catch Highway 224 that paralleled the Clackamas River, then take 46 to Detroit. After that we'd figure it out.

We grabbed a bite in Estacada, then followed the river. A ministry mentor had lived on the Clackamas farther downstream and I knew its beauty, but that increased as we journeyed upstream. A lot of stops along it made me wish I'd brought a trout rod, but this was a biking trip. The road then turned to the south, and we began climbing. Lush evergreens hemmed us in, and we got a little snow alongside, then we came to a major obstacle. Snow covered most of the road, and a tree had fallen across, blocking a clear path. But we'd seen another biker come down a few miles before, so we figured the route was clear. We cautiously slipped through a small opening in the pine branches. More snow, but the road was good enough . . . until we reached a steel gate with a road closed sign. The first sign Oregon roads had provided. I checked—no lock, so we could open it. Do we risk it? We walked ahead a little only to find snow covered the road: impassable.

We had to retrace our entire route back to Jerry's house. Were we annoyed that Oregon didn't post a road closed sign earlier? You bet your bippy. I thought of the verse in Corinthians about how God always leads in triumph; that helped. Besides, every road looks different going in the opposite direction. We gained a fresh perspective on a lot of beautiful country. And we saved the cost of a motel room.

Robert Burns said it well: "The best laid plans of mice and men often go astray." A pretty wise and gifted poet who knew that life turns and twists in unexpected manners. One of my go-to phrases has become, "It is what it is." Reality supersedes our plans and dreams and fantasies. The key comes when we realize that despite everything, we don't always get our way. Why?

Sometimes, God steps in to change our plans. One of my life verses promises, "We can make our plans, *but the Lord* determines our steps" (Proverbs 16:9 NLT). God knows far more than we, loves people and us far more than we, and has a plan for life that surpasses ours. I'm making it a habit to say thank you when something I've planned or wanted and prayed for changed. With the benefit of looking back, I've often realized that God knew better and directed my steps. Accepting Jesus as Lord gives him the freedom to intervene for the best.

The choices of others can change our plans, because God grants free choice to all, and choices have consequences. We can control our responses but not all that happens. One prayer for a promotion was given to someone else by my boss. My family historical novel *Wild Rides* delves into the reality of people negatively affecting others. My paternal great grandfather and his son, my grandfather, left a trail of damaged people in their wake: just one realized that and tried to make it right.

And sometimes life, or coincidence, steps in. Jesus told of some who had plans for their lives until the tower of Siloam collapsed and killed them. Why? They had done nothing wrong, but were just in the wrong place at the wrong time (Luke 13:1–5).

So when plans change, what do we do? We remember that God always loves us and comforts us: "You have made known to me the paths of life; you will *fill me with joy in your presence*" (Acts 2:28). Yes, plans change, crap happens, but no damage can match the joy we have knowing the awesome Creator of the universe is with us. Every step of the way.

Because of his love, God takes the next step: "And we know that *in all things God works* for the good of those who love him, who have been called according to his purpose" (Romans 8:28). God does that when we choose to accept his purpose for us. We may not be aware of his working until we look backward, but we trust in his presence and work.

So let's look ahead, evaluate the options, count the cost, and make our plans, knowing that God works for our spiritual good whatever happens. We can relax, knowing God has our best in mind.

DAY THIRTY-FIVE

Kick-Starting the Application

How much do you plan your life? How committed are you to those? When your plans go astray, do you get upset and frown or do you smile? How much do you involve God in your plans and results?

DAY THIRTY-SIX

START SLOW

Speed's Way

I never expected to realize my lifelong dream of driving a Lamborghini—no rich friends who had one, and one certainly wouldn't fit our budget. Then I heard of Exotics Racing, at the AAA track in Fontana, where you could buy some laps on a road course. Sheila graciously agreed to combine several birthday and Christmas gifts, so I made the reservation.

That led to researching the Lambo that Exotics used, the Gallardo 550. I figured it was like my smartphone: more capabilities than I could hope to use. And while I used and enjoyed clutches, the Lambo had a paddle shifter, so I researched that.

Almost foolishly, I expected them to hand me the keys on arriving at the track. But no, we had an hour class with videos. How to paddle shift—we didn't have to worry about the tach, the onboard coach would tell us when to shift; that shortened the learning curve. They spent time on cornering—don't hug the inside edge as I'd always done, but make just two turns. They showed a diagram to help grasp it, a longer way around the curve but faster. High school geometry helped me understand it.

They told us not to accelerate full speed out of the curve, which could cause a skid that might change the car's alignment. Yes, I did skid a little once. We would have one other car on the track, and if one came up behind us, the instructor would tap our shoulder and we'd slow down more and move to the right.

They told some stories to help out. One driver complained of soreness in his forearms after his run. The instructor smiled and said, "You gripped the wheel too tight. Be firm but not tense." Mine were fine—I learned from it. But the amount of concentration it required surprised me, even with the instructor helping a lot.

Then they piled us into a Porsche SUV for two laps around the track, where the driver told and showed us how to set up for a turn, how to always have our foot on the gas or the brake, and never to coast. That increases your lap time. They encouraged us to go slow the first two laps to get a feel for the car and course. The two extra laps I purchased paid off.

I was blown away at all that was involved in going fast on a road course. Jerry and I had visited the Laguna Seca Raceway in the Bay Area and seen a Ferrari race car; the steering wheel was *not* a wheel but a scientific device, controlling dozens of functions. Before acting in a race movie, Paul Newman took race training at a school and raced smaller vehicles for three years before his first pro race.

And here I was, taking on a bull of a supercar on a twisty course with an hour of training. My admiration for racers grew by orders of magnitude.

God's Way

Entering Pepperdine as a Bible major, my academic adviser told me they required a speech course. "But I have a debate scholarship. Could I take a homiletics or preaching class instead?" With a nice smile he responded, "Ready to go out and save the world?"

I said yes, but I soon realized I wasn't. My genuine but shallow faith evaporated in that first year. Four years of searching brought me back to a relationship with God, and I took some classes at another Christian college to deepen my faith and knowledge. Then, almost two years later, a church in Torrance hired me as their part-time youth pastor.

After a slow start, I arrived at ready, yet that process of "getting more ready" still continues.

Most who read this book aren't apt to take a supercar on a road course nor enter the professional ministry. But two key principles, growth and service, apply to all who follow Jesus, and we begin them when we follow. I had driven fast before, but needed training to optimize the Lambo. In these two, we start slow and grow to become more spiritually optimized.

God intended that we grow. Growth takes time. We get salvation when we commit our lives to Jesus as Savior and Lord. But that begins the process; it doesn't end it: "Continue to *work out your salvation* with fear and trembling, for it is *God who works in you to will* and *to act* according to his good purpose" (Philippians 2:12–13).

When we work out with weights, we gain no new muscles—they merely grow as we exercise what we already have. We cooperate with the God who works in us, who has a plan for our character, and who works in us. But we need to do our part. We get to know his word. We rely on him to do what we cannot. And the more we grow, the more effective we become when we serve.

God gave all followers the mission of affecting people, of making disciples (Matthew 28:18–20) and gifts us with differing abilities and resources. Read Matthew 25:14–30 on your own; it tells of an owner who gave his servants (us) differing amounts while he went on a journey. When he returned he rewarded those who used their gifts for him and condemned the one who did nothing.

The tremendously gifted Paul spent three years in Arabia, alone, after his conversion before beginning his ministry. He started slow. Now, do we start serving as soon as we're saved? Of course. But let's not rush so much that we don't develop our faith and our skills.

At Fontana, without my preparation through my research, the class, and the two slow laps, I never could have reached 112 miles per hour on that course. Taking the time to prep allowed me to take better advantage of the Lambo's abilities. A good goal for us all in our walk with Jesus.

Kick Starting the Application

How intentionally do you develop your faith and service? How can you increase it? What areas might be best to focus on?

DAY THIRTY-SEVEN

LAUNCHED BY A BIKE

Rich Klinsky

Rich Klinsky lives in Huron, South Dakota, with his wife, Gayle. He spends his time doting on his grandkids and enjoying his motorcycles—when the weather is nice. He has been involved with CMA (Christian Motorcycle Association) for over 10 years and likes the fellowship it provides.

I got my first bike at 17, a green Honda 350 Scrambler, a cross between street and dirt bikes. I've enjoyed riding ever since and have had many bikes over the decades. Soon after, Tim picked up a similar 1970 blue Scrambler, and we took a lot of rides up past Mount Wilson to a summer camp we went to. Along the way I added a Harley Sportster, and sometimes I'd loan my 350 to Jerry Christensen, another author in this book, and I'd ride my Harley. They raced; I cruised.

We've enjoyed many riding trips together since then, the most recent one being six years ago when we rode through much of British Columbia to Alaska and back in eight days! We saw some glaciers and some bears, and got really wet.

Throughout my life God has spared me in several life-threatening circumstances. I've had items fall off the back of trucks in front of me on the freeway of Los Angeles. I've been caught in rip tides in the ocean. I've had people hit their brakes in front of me and slide sideways on rain-slicked roads. The angels were there when I needed them.

The worst scenario happened when I center-punched a car at 50 miles an hour. When I was 26 years old, returning home from work at General Motors in South Gate, California, a driver wasn't paying attention and turned left in front of me, and I unintentionally T-boned him on the right passenger side door. The impact decimated my front tire and bent the front forks into the frame of my motorcycle.

This sent me flying over the car's passenger compartment, and the angels took over. I rolled once in the intersection and ended up standing on the street corner, looking at my crumpled bike in the intersection. The glasses I had on were old and loose; they used to fall off if I simply looked down. They somehow remained on my face the entire time.

In this accident, I didn't have a single wound on my body. I was somehow untouched, except for road burn on each elbow and knee—not even a tear in my clothing. No option but a miracle. A little boy saw the whole thing happen, and he looked up at me, his eyes as big as saucers. I asked him if I could borrow his skateboard, and without saying a word he handed it to me.

The driver had long since vanished; he must not have had insurance, and bailed. So I took the skateboard to the motorcycle and got it upright, put the mangled front wheel on top of the skateboard, and rolled it to the side of the road. I went to the corner house, rang the doorbell, and asked if I could use their phone. I called my wife, Gayle, and she came to pick me up. Twice in one day, God sent an angel to rescue me.

California then didn't require helmets, and Rich wasn't wearing one. Get this: a sudden stop, vaulted the car, rolled just once, landed on his feet, and never banged his vulnerable head on the car nor asphalt. I commented, "Rich, you don't get many miracles in this life . . . might be time to start wearing a brain bucket more often."

No doubt an angel guided Rich on his launch and landing. I experienced that as well in Canada when the chain slipped and locked the rear wheel on a curve. That's in the first book, *God, a Motorcycle, and the Open Road*, in the chapter "When Angels Ride Along."

But I also have friends who died in bike accidents, others who were in serious accidents that left them disabled. So why does God miraculously intervene at times and not at others?

I don't know. He doesn't give me an answer to all my questions, and I still have a lot. But a finite human fully comprehending an infinite deity is like an ant critiquing Einstein's theory of relativity. Ain't gonna happen.

But we can glean some insights on dealing with this issue. Will it give all the answers? No. Will it give some help? I pray so.

The foundation must begin with a conviction that in all things, God loves us unconditionally and he acts: "For God so loved the world that he gave his one and only Son" (John 3:16). He never abandons us.

Out of that love, he trusts us with our ability to choose, real choices with real consequences: "*You are free* to eat from any tree in the garden; *but* you must not eat from the tree of the knowledge of good and evil, for *when you eat of it you will certainly die*" (Genesis 2:16–17). Our choices bring good and bad, to ourselves and others. Often, to innocent and undeserving others. My first novel, *Wild Rides*, explores those consequences.

Let's keep in mind that we humans brought evil into our world. God works against it.

We often hear "everything happens for a reason," to which one wit added, "And sometimes that reason is your bad choices." I would add, maybe because of somebody else's choice. God's will is not always done; every choice to sin violates his will: "It is *God's will* that you should *be sanctified*" (1 Thessalonians 4:3). Not all people are.

So maybe we need to avoid blaming God and instead focus on our next best step in handling reality. Romans 8:28 gives us guidance:

"And we know that *in all things God works* for the good of those who love him" (). Things don't work for good; God does. Will the hard times end? Maybe, maybe not. But the God who loved us enough to give his Son won't abandon us.

Maybe we can cling to that.

Kick-Starting the Application

Have you struggled with God allowing hard times in your life? Did you focus on the good things God has done for you in love? How have your bad choices contributed to your difficulties?

DAY THIRTY-EIGHT

A TIME TO SLOW DOWN: IT CAN SAVE YOUR LIFE

For our audacious 2022 East Coast trip of 8,500 miles to add the last states to our tallies, Jerry and I planned to meet on a Sunday in Green River, Utah, then exit Utah, pass through Colorado, and move on to Kansas and points east. From Temecula, Green River lay 690 miles distant, a little more than this old body preferred to do in one day. Yeah, times have changed. I left Saturday morning covering 580 miles before reaching a motel in Salida, Utah. Not my preferred place, but it worked out mile wise. On a similar trip the next year, I stopped 20 miles earlier in Richfield. I'd recommend that.

Jerry had nearly 1,000 miles, so he left his home in the Salem, Oregon, area on Friday, did a tough 630 miles to spend his first night in Burley, Idaho, and arrived in Green River Saturday afternoon after a more relaxed day of 365 miles.

Saturday called for me to ride 110 miles, about an hour and half, to meet him. Being eager to get together, I geared up early for a cold morning and hit the road on my Goldwing, maybe exceeding what I recall as an 80-mile-per-hour speed limit. The temp on the bike read 30 when I left, but 20 miles later it dropped to 17 on a pass of almost 8,000 feet. But the Wing gave great protection, and it just loafed along through the countryside route featuring all green dots on the map, with majestic scenery overlooking the Capitol and San Rafael Reefs, where Butch Cassidy and his gang spent some time.

Butch fascinates this amateur historian, so I just had to stop and take a few pics They often hid out in their Robbers' Roost in those rugged mesas, and I've toured his family cabin in Circleville, Utah.

That stop slowed me down a bit, so I hopped back on the bike and kicked it up to 85. Within a few miles, I almost lost control. I entered a sweeping curve and set my line, only to quickly brake and swerve to avoid an unexpected pothole. The asphalt was in rough shape—potholes and bumps and bad tar patches. Continuing at my speed on those road conditions could be deadly; no one could keep a safe line on the curves while dodging the obstacles.

So I grudgingly dropped 30 miles an hour off my speed. It turns out the road ahead had the same asphalt difficulties for another 10 miles or so, and I realized it was time to slow down. Yes, that bothered me. The curves had been well designed. I like taking advantage of the Wing's power and stability and cornering, and that road suited 85 miles per hour . . . on good pavement, which this was not. But realizing it is what it is, I adapted. Yes, I arrived a little later than I hoped. But I arrived alive. In adjusting to reality, sometimes we need to slow down.

I tend to have a high completion quotient—liking to get a task done as soon as possible, in part to avoid my inclination toward procrastination. I've been a fool who rushed in too quickly where angels fear to tread. Patience does not come naturally to me, and some of my biggest life decisions were made in utter spontaneity. Some of my best decisions, some of my worst. So here are some suggestions from one who continues to learn—the hard way—the importance of going slow.

First, patience represents the heart and nature of God: "The fruit of the Spirit is . . . *patience*" (Galatians 5:22 BSB). Think of the patience he exerted in crafting the universe—over billions of years. Think of his patience from the entry of sin in the garden until Jesus brought redemption. Now the bad news: Patience literally means long-suffering. Hanging in during difficulties and not bailing too soon. Realizing that growth takes time.

DAY THIRTY-EIGHT

Do you desire enough spiritual maturity to soar? Then slow down: "Those who *wait on the* LORD shall renew their strength; They shall mount up with wings like eagles" (Isaiah 40:31 NKJV). The word *wait* is an active participle, meaning to look for in the future, to expect. We don't wait passively; it takes repeated decisions to do it. But we build strength as we wait on God in patience. Sometimes with suffering. But slowing down to wait on God to act benefits us.

Second, we go slow to allow God to set the schedule. In the early 600s BC, Judah under Josiah was threatened by a changing dynamic among the world powers, and Judah had little power on their own. The prophet Zephaniah, a contemporary of Isaiah, told God's people, "'Therefore *wait for me*,' declares the LORD, 'for the day I will stand up to testify. I have decided to assemble the nations'" (Zephaniah 3:8). Basically, God said, "I've got this. Just sit back and watch. Don't mess it up by getting in my way." He's God, and we're not.

I wonder how much of our impatience comes from not trusting God to do his God stuff. Do we sometimes think God needs our help to speed up the program? Perhaps the best tool to build patience is to say, "God, you have this. I can rest."

Kick-Starting the Application

Do you tend to rush into plans or procrastinate? Have you been burned by going too fast? What area might you need to slow down in right now?

DAY THIRTY-NINE

CARS I HAVE LOVED AND LOST

E. Wayne Kempton

Wayne combines being an author, attorney, retired pastor, federal special agent, and an inveterate lover of sports cars.

Speed's Way

My wife Shari did not dare look out our window at the new Datsun 240Z. The dealer had let us take the Z-Car home while the finance company decided about taking a risk on us. It seemed dicey. My Marine Corps enlistment would end in two months, and we had planned for me to work at a grocery store while finishing college and, later, law school. But the desired job fell through, and my sweet Shari was pregnant.

The next day, the finance company decided we were worth the risk. "It won't hurt much, will it?" was Shari's concern about the finances.

Four months later, all worked out. I obtained a full-time job at a grocery store while attending college full-time.

Even more joy soon arrived: Our first child was due any moment. Once Shari's labor began, she and I jumped in the Z-Car, heading to the hospital for our first baby. During the drive, Shari hopefully and bravely said, "It won't hurt much, will it?"

Many hours later, we were blessed with a breath-taking miracle—a sweet little girl named Heather. As I drove our two-seat Z-Car home,

Shari held baby Heather in her arms; there were no laws against such things back in those days.

Four years later, our son Jeffrey came along. Just as with Heather's birth, I drove Shari to the hospital. But this time held no, "It won't hurt much, will it?" And just like with Heather, we drove home from Jeffrey's birth with Shari holding her baby boy in her arms. In the Z-Car.

We owned the Z-Car for 18 joyous years. After law school, we drove our beautiful car to Washington, DC, to begin my career as a Special Agent. Four years later, on our return to California, our Z-Car looked sadly different: the salt on the highways in the winters back east rusted her out. When we drove the Z-Car home, she ran great . . . but she was an eyesore.

We gave up our beloved Z-Car in 1990 when I was assigned to the US Embassy in Germany. We moved there as a family of four, including two teenagers. We had an allowance to ship only one car, so we had to bring a four-door car to hold our whole family. Sadly, after 18 years, we bid adieu to the Z-Car.

On my farewell trip in the Z-Car up to Santa Barbara, I swore she purred as nicely as she did on the day I first drove her off the showroom floor. On the day I sold her, as I watched her going away down our street for the last time, I struggled just as much looking at the cherished Z-Car as Shari had on the day we bought her.

Oh, and my official government car in Germany was a 12-cylinder Jaguar . . . just to ease the pain. The Jag was no sports car, but it was a great, swift Autobahn cruiser.

God's Way

Wayne, so far, has owned 22 cars, half of which qualify as sporty—that's a lot of cars to say goodbye to, some sad partings, like to his beloved Z-Car. I think all of us who love cars and bikes grieve at losing some of ours.

DAY THIRTY-NINE

As I learned in history class, "change is the only constant in life," and the huge increase of digital change factored into my decision to retire at 67. My dad's birth came less than one year before the novel Wright brothers' flight and four years before the Model T. Well before he passed, men walked on the moon and traversed the continent in a matter of hours.

Frankly, change can bewilder and put us off. Hence, Shari's repeated haunting phrase, "Will it hurt?" Our culture seems overpowered by change, and most Americans believe we're going in the wrong direction. Morality gets determined by each individual. Some Days in our book explore navigating change, so let's go deeper. Can we find a foundation, a north star, that we can rely on in life? Something that doesn't change?

Here's the exception to my history prof: God. "Before the mountains were born or You brought forth the earth and the world, *from everlasting to everlasting You are God*" (Psalm 90:2 BSB). God has been God—forever in the past, forever in the future: "I the LORD *do not change*" (Malachi 3:6). So in a world that's constantly changing and rearranging, we have an unchanging bedrock to rely on. As Creator, he has the credibility that can be trusted. And this comes with two very practical benefits to us.

Grab onto this unchanging result: "But from everlasting to everlasting the *LORD's love* is with those who fear him" (Psalm 103:17a). Because love resides in the nature of our unchanging God, we can rest easy that he cares. Nothing in all creation can separate us from that love (Romans 8:38–39). Yes, difficulties still arise, but God lovingly stays with us.

The end of that psalm verse gives another benefit: "But from everlasting to everlasting the *LORD's . . . righteousness* [is] with their children's children" (Psalm 103:17b). Because God doesn't change like shifting sands, he pours his righteousness into those who fear him, and they can build a family heritage of righteousness. We can end family cycles of disfunction and sin. The same God when we were young is that same God our grandchildren can experience.

So in a world of constant and sometimes fearful change, God remains. The same. Forever. Good news for us.

Crossing the Finish Line

Do you tend to embrace or resist change? Do you sometimes find yourself stunned by it? Have you thought of the benefits of an unchanging God? Which touches you the most?

DAY FORTY

AND SO IT ENDED: ONE CRAP-OUT AND ONE CRASH

In life, many seemingly minor issues grow in importance. I thought my first long ride from SoCal to Canada in 1970 would be a one-off. Just one-day rides after. Then a mission trip to the Taos, New Mexico, area came up. Two of us rode there, so I swapped my well-used 350 for an almost-new 750 semi-chopped Honda Easy Rider bike. At the end of month-long time, a wild hair of an idea sent me east to see family in Nashville; I was halfway there!

The mission trip repeated in '74. I'd quit my job just before and had a wilder idea to see America—a very troubled America during Watergate and Vietnam. Those two months on a solo ride changed my life, covering 31 states and 13,000 miles. Out of curiosity I added it up, 40 states in total. About then getting all 50 on a bike approached bucket-list status. On a trip to Hawaii, I bagged it on a borrowed bike; a friend, Rich Klinsky, helped me get Alaska; another friend, Jerry Christensen, helped get the Upper Midwest from North Dakota to Wisconsin; and with the Gray Hogs riding over the West the total hit 47.

That turned it into a bucket list, needing just Florida, Georgia, and South Carolina. Then faithful Jerry suggested a trip to the Southeast to get those. I agreed, then he said his daughter lives just north in Maryland, so could we see them? I couldn't say no. Then Jerry kept thinking; he got out a map and worked out a route that would go up to Maine, then west, and he would have all 48 and I'd get my last 3.

In May 2022, we two old guys in our mid-70s headed off on an 8,000-ride. Audacious! But we were eager and could do it on 400-mile days in under three weeks. Some Days in this book have dealt with that trip. We saw country we'd never seen before, visited some places we only heard about. But maybe 3,000 miles in, some issues arose. Some friction with my long-time best friend (mostly due to me), some miscommunication, some close calls, and I began to get a vague sense of unease. Was that a whisper from God or doubt from Satan? But we soldiered on.

Frustration came as we tried to bypass NYC, but we found a nice hotel in Fairfield, Connecticut, with the Maine border about 370 miles away—a one-day ride, then we'd head west, and get his 48. Then head home.

I led onto the I-95 onramp in Fairfield, then noticed Jerry wasn't behind me, so I stopped after the next off ramp and called. His Can Am had died on him and wouldn't restart. That had happened once before in Oregon. So I got off and headed south to get below his onramp, but it took me to the one above him. I did that three times so figured I'd go north and circle back and go south to get well below him.

Following the signs, I came to a dead end. Left wouldn't work, so I turned right, came to a stop sign, stopped, looked, and moved into the intersection, only to have a passenger van appear out of nowhere, and I struck him.

My yellow Wing bled green coolant and black oil; the forks got twisted terribly. I merely had a scrape on my elbow. The first responders suggested I sue; this was the most dangerous intersection in the state.

And so the audacious ride ended, one bike crapped out, one totaled. Jerry, unable to trust his, sold it the next day to a bike shop, took the train to his daughter's home in Maryland, and flew home. I rented a car and drove home, stopping to see my sis in Kentucky.

But was God behind it? Did we ignore his earlier hints in our ambition to achieve the states? Only he knows, but I wonder.

That's not all of the story. Jerry hoped, and I agreed, to try again the next year, a shorter ride. But on his first day, Jerry felt leg pain when he woke up, rode 600 miles to Idaho, and couldn't continue. He headed home, felt better in a day, so we ended up doing some day rides in Oregon. But I wonder. It truly seems like God, for some reason that we have no clue about, didn't want us to finish the trip.

Never before or after have I felt such unease on a trip. Never before have two consecutive rides been wiped out. That's why this passage came to mind, both when it happened, and as I write this:

> Paul and his companions traveled throughout the region of Phrygia and Galatia, having been *kept by the Holy Spirit* from preaching the word in the province of Asia. When they came to the border of Mysia, they tried to enter Bithynia, but the *Spirit of Jesus would not allow them* to. So they passed by Mysia and went down to Troas. During the night *Paul had a vision* of a man of Macedonia standing and begging him, "Come over to Macedonia and help us." After Paul had seen the vision, we got ready at once to leave for Macedonia, concluding that God had called us to preach the gospel to them. (Acts 16:6–10)

God does warn his people. He does guide and direct us. So what might have been his purpose in ending our trip, if in fact he did? Just some guesses. Continuing could have risked our lives; a worse accident might have occurred. Or it could have been that he had another purpose for us, like he did with Paul in Troas. It could be that he wanted us, and now you, to be sensitive to the hints of the Spirit. I do believe he ended that quest. So now, I try to listen more carefully.

Kick-Starting the Application

Have you heard the soft whisper of God? How did you respond? How can you listen more attentively?